Cambridge Elements ≡

Elements in Perception
edited by
James T. Enns
The University of British Columbia

VISUAL CONTROL OF LOCOMOTION

Brett R. Fajen
Rensselaer Polytechnic Institute

CAMBRIDGE
UNIVERSITY PRESS

CAMBRIDGE
UNIVERSITY PRESS

University Printing House, Cambridge CB2 8BS, United Kingdom

One Liberty Plaza, 20th Floor, New York, NY 10006, USA

477 Williamstown Road, Port Melbourne, VIC 3207, Australia

314–321, 3rd Floor, Plot 3, Splendor Forum, Jasola District Centre, New Delhi – 110025, India

79 Anson Road, #06–04/06, Singapore 079906

Cambridge University Press is part of the University of Cambridge.

It furthers the University's mission by disseminating knowledge in the pursuit of education, learning, and research at the highest international levels of excellence.

www.cambridge.org
Information on this title: www.cambridge.org/9781108799270
DOI: 10.1017/9781108870474

First published 2021

A catalogue record for this publication is available from the British Library.

ISBN 978-1-108-79927-0 Paperback
ISSN 2515-0502 (online)
ISSN 2515-0499 (print)

Additional resources for this publication at www.cambridge.org/fajen

Visual Control of Locomotion

Elements in Perception

DOI:10.1017/9781108870474
First published online: March 2021

Brett R. Fajen
Rensselaer Polytechnic Institute

Author for correspondence: Brett R. Fajen, fajenb@rpi.edu

Abstract: This Element examines visual perception in the context of activities that involve moving about in complex, dynamic environments. A central theme is that the ability of humans and other animals to perceive their surroundings based on vision is profoundly shaped by the need to adaptively regulate locomotion to variations in the environment. As such, important new insights into what and how we perceive can be gleaned by investigating the connection between vision and the control of locomotion. I present an integrated summary of decades of research on the perception of self-motion and object motion based on optic flow, the perception of spatial layout and affordances, and the control strategies for guiding locomotion based on visual information. I also explore important theoretical issues and debates, including the question of whether visual control relies on internal models.

Keywords: locomotion, visual control, optic flow, affordance perception

ISBNs:9781108799270 (PB), 9781108870474 (OC)
ISSNs:2515-0502 (online), 2515-0499 (print)

Contents

1 Introduction   1

2 Optic Flow and the Perception of Self-Motion   2

3 Perception of Spatial Layout and Affordances by an
Active Observer   24

4 Strategies for Online Visual Control   34

5 The Internal-Model Debate   47

6 Concluding Remarks   56

References   58

1 Introduction

At its core, perception is the means by which humans, other forms of life, and arguably certain kinds of machines come to know about and be in contact with their surroundings. It plays a fundamental role in almost all daily activities, but there is perhaps no more universal example of the absolute necessity of perceptual contact with one's surroundings than moving through complex, dynamic environments. Almost all naturalistic behaviors involve moving the body from one location to another within spaces that contain hazards such as stationary and moving obstacles and surfaces that are uneven, unstable, or slippery. Perception makes it possible for us to negotiate these hazards and to safely and efficiently accomplish goals that require movement of the body.

To better appreciate this point, imagine starting your day with an early morning trail run through a serene forest. After a short stretch of flat, well-packed earth, you encounter a small creek. You immediately see that the creek is narrow enough to leap across but also notice that the rocks on the far side are too rounded, smooth, and damp to keep you from slipping when you land. Fortunately, there is a flat, dry rock in the middle of the stream protruding above the surface of the water. It is narrow, but with a carefully aimed step, your foot hits its target and within another step you are back on the trail. A few minutes later, you come across a large tree limb that has fallen across the trail. You could step off the trail and walk around, but instead you quickly accelerate and hurdle the branch. Over the next 10 minutes, the trail thins out and is often difficult to distinguish from the surrounding forest. You shift your gaze from tree to tree as you continue running, looking for trail markers, but occasionally gaze downward to detect tree roots and rocks that would otherwise have caused you to stumble. Toward the end of your run, the trail crosses over a road. You spot an approaching car but immediately see that you are able to reach the other side before the car arrives.

What is demanded of perception as you faced each of these challenges? If you have taken a course on perception, you can readily appreciate that successfully negotiating such terrain relies on many of the perceptual capabilities that you learned about, such as perceiving the spatial layout of the scene, perceiving the identity, shape, and surface properties of objects, perceiving motion, and selectively attending to task-relevant properties of the environment. Yet each of these basic perceptual capabilities is seen in a new light when carefully reexamined in the context of activities that involve locomotion. Even fundamental assumptions about the job of perception and the kinds of properties that are assumed to be the objects of perception are brought into question.

Over the past few decades, the idea that perception and action are intertwined and that one cannot be fully understood without the other has gained considerable traction among perceptual scientists. Yet this awareness is not well reflected in most textbooks used in introductory perception courses, which still treat the role of perception in the control of action as an afterthought. This Element was written to fill this gap and to help readers understand perception as a process that has been shaped by the need of animals to move about in cluttered environments.

Section 2 introduces readers to the analysis of information that is available to moving observers in the form of optic flow. It also examines what is known about how such information is used to perceive one's movement through the environment as well as the movement of other objects. Section 3 examines the perception of spatial layout by active observers and the perception of possibilities for action (i.e., affordances). In the remaining sections, the focus shifts from perception to control. In Section 4, I discuss how visual information is used to control and guide action in the context of various locomotor tasks and consider various theoretical perspectives on the linkage between visual perception and action. Section 5 examines the question of whether the control of locomotion relies on internal models, which has sparked a great deal of controversy and has shaped a considerable amount of research on this topic over the past few decades. Readers who are interested in only one of these topics can read individual sections on their own with the exception of Section 5, which should be read after Section 4.

Although multiple sensory modalities contribute to the control of locomotion, the primary focus of this Element is on vision and how it allows one to guide locomotion in an anticipatory manner. This is not to diminish the importance of the vestibular and somatosensory systems. These systems also play key roles in the control of locomotion, especially in the reactive responses that are needed to maintain stability following perturbations. Readers who are interested in the multisensory contributions to self-motion perception and control are referred to reviews by Cullen (2019), Greenlee, Frank, Kaliuzhna, Blanke, Bremmer, Churan, Cuturi, MacNeilage, and Smith (2016), and Israël and Warren (2005).

2 Optic Flow and the Perception of Self-Motion

2.1 The Optic Flow Field

As one moves through the environment, the pattern of light surrounding the observer changes in a systematic way. These changing patterns are known as optic flow and they provide the moving observer with a rich source of information about both their movement through the world and the structure of the environment.

To build your intuitions about optic flow, imagine that you are out for a ride on your bike and traveling on a long, straight bike path with no other cars, cyclists, or pedestrians in view. Figure 1A depicts the optical motion similar to what you would encounter as you travel down the path. The white lines trace the changing locations on the image of stationary objects in the environment as the cyclist moves forward. Whereas the lines in Figure 1A capture the image motion over several frames, the optical motion at any instant can be represented as a two-dimensional velocity vector field $V(x, y)$, where the direction and magnitude of motion at each point or pixel is represented by a vector (see Figure 1B). Inspecting Figure 1B, one is immediately struck by the presence of a globally coherent pattern – specifically, a radial expansion reminiscent of the celebrated jump to warp speed in *Star Wars*. This global transformation of the optic array is a direct consequence of your forward motion on the bike and is a paradigmatic example of what James J. Gibson referred to as the optic flow field.

Gibson coined this term in the 1940s (Gibson, 1950; Reed, 1988) while he was conducting research for the United States Air Force on how to evaluate and train pilots to land aircraft. Although the project started with a focus on pilots' visual capabilities, Gibson quickly realized that more could be learned by studying the perceptual information available to pilots. This led to a detailed analysis of the structure of the global pattern of optical motion surrounding the

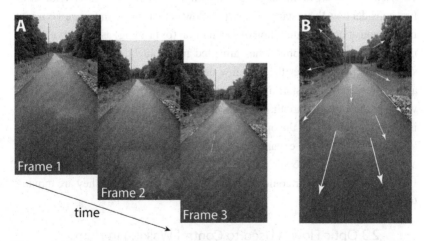

Figure 1 (A) Three frames of video depicting linear self-motion through a static environment. Circles track image positions of elements across frames. (B) Optic flow field represented as a velocity vector field. Color version of figure available at www.cambridge.org/fajen

moving observer as well as how that structure provides information about the environment and the observer's movement within it (Gibson, Olum, & Rosenblatt, 1955).

Over the years, many researchers have sought to identify potential sources of information in optic flow. Such analyses have proven to be useful starting points upon which to build accounts of the visual control of locomotion, for the problem that organisms face in controlling locomotion is to a large degree shaped by the available information. Section 2 introduces readers to this body of research. By the end of this section, readers will possess the intuitions needed to understand how optic flow depends on the movement of the observer and the structure of the environment, be able to identify the main sources of information that are available to moving observers and relevant to the control of locomotion, and be familiar with experimental research designed to determine which sources of information observers actually use to perceive the world and their motion through it. Readers are also encouraged to check out one or more of the excellent review papers on optic flow (e.g., Warren, 1995; Warren, 1998a; Warren, 2004; Lappe, Bremmer, & Van den Berg, 1999), which collectively summarize work on this topic through the early 2000s. Section 2 of this Element builds upon these papers, with an emphasis on developments in this area over the past 15 years.

2.2 Heading Direction and Information in Optic Flow

To orient the reader to the analysis of information in the optic flow field, let us first consider how the instantaneous optic flow field depicted in Figure 1B might inform you about your direction of locomotion (or heading) as you travel down the bike path. This problem has attracted much attention within the vision science community over the past few decades and continues to be an active area of research. The starting point is the singularity in the optic flow field, which in the case of smooth, forward locomotion through a static environment is the point from which the optical motion in Figure 1B radiates. This feature is known as the focus of expansion (FoE) and is of significance because of its alignment with the observer's direction of heading. Therefore, by locating the FoE, a moving observer could perceive the direction in which they are moving (Gibson, 1950).

2.3 Optic Flow Is Used to Control Walking in Humans

Gibson (1950) also proposed that optic flow could be used to guide locomotion. To steer your bike through an opening between two parked cars, for example, you could move in such a way as to align the FoE with the opening. If the FoE is to the left or the right of the opening, you should adjust your direction of travel until the two are aligned. By continuing to maintain alignment while moving forward, you will eventually reach the opening.

Gibson's hypothesis was the catalyst for a great deal of research (some of which is summarized below) on the perception of heading from optic flow. Nevertheless, it should not be taken for granted that optic flow is actually used to steer toward a goal. After all, humans are capable of walking to a target in the absence of optic flow. You can demonstrate this fact to yourself by asking a friend to illuminate a small penlight in an otherwise completely dark and empty room and attempting to walk toward the light. Assuming that there are no obstacles in the way, you should have no trouble aligning yourself and walking to the target. In spite of the absence of optic flow, humans can easily perform this task by perceiving the visual direction of the target in a body-centric reference frame (i.e., the egocentric direction) and walking in that direction (Rushton, Harris, Lloyd, & Wann, 1998). If humans are capable of using egocentric direction to guide locomotion to a goal when optic flow is absent, then perhaps they also use egocentric direction when optic flow is present.

The definitive test of the egocentric direction and optic flow hypotheses was a study by Warren, Kay, Zosh, Duchon, and Sahuc (2001) that was conducted in a virtual environment. Using a clever virtual reality manipulation, the authors offset the optic flow from the direction in which subjects walked, creating a situation in which the use of an optic flow strategy would require following a straight path to the goal, and the use of an egocentric direction strategy would require following a curved path to the goal. When the only object in the virtual environment was a thin target line (i.e., in the absence of optic flow), subjects walked along a curved trajectory consistent with the use of egocentric direction. As more visual structure (and hence richer optic flow) was added to the virtual environment, the trajectory became more linear. Importantly, in the latter case, both optic flow and egocentric direction are available but in conflict. The fact that subjects walked on a nearly straight path to the goal led the authors to conclude that optic flow dominates visual direction. Thus, the findings support Gibson's hypothesis and motivate further investigation of optic flow, information therein, and its role in the perception and control of self-motion.

2.4 Perceiving Heading and Path from Optic Flow

2.4.1 Heading Perception during Translational Self-Motion

Although Gibson's ideas about optic flow originated during the middle part of the twentieth century, it was not until the late 1980s that research on this topic began to take off. Developments in computer graphics technology during this period made it possible for vision scientists to create and manipulate optic flow stimuli for psychophysical testing. One of the most basic questions that one could ask is how accurately observers can judge their direction of self-motion based on optic flow. Here we must make a distinction between the perception of self-motion relative to objects in the world (which is sometimes referred to as the path perception) and the perception of self-motion in an egocentric reference frame (e.g., relative to the direction that the eyes, head, or body are facing). For the simplest case involving linear self-motion through a static environment, human observers can perceive their path relative to objects in the world with discrimination thresholds of less than 1° of visual angle. This was demonstrated by presenting subjects with brief visual stimuli simulating self-motion followed by a probe positioned to one side of the actual self-motion direction by a small amount and instructing subjects to judge whether they would pass to the left or the right of the probe (Warren, Morris, & Kalish, 1988). The perception of heading direction in an egocentric reference frame is considerably less accurate and subject to systematic biases. Cuturi and MacNeilage (2013) presented subjects with visual and vestibular stimuli simulating self-motion across a wide range of directions (360°) and instructed them to orient a pointer in the perceived direction of self-motion. They found that heading angles were over-estimated by as much as 10° (e.g., moving 45° to the right of straight ahead was judged as moving by as much as 55° to the right). The relevance of such biases for the perception and control of locomotion is a topic that deserves more consideration. Cuturi and MacNeilage propose that these distortions in heading perception could actually be functional. Small errors around straight ahead are perceptually magnified, which could allow for more precise estimation in the range of heading directions that is most relevant to the guidance of locomotion. On the other hand, for tasks that involve guiding locomotion relative to objects in the world, the significance of such perceptual biases is unclear.

Importantly, the use of optic flow to perceive self-motion direction does not necessarily require that the focus of expansion be visible. In principle, the location of the FoE can be recovered by sampling any small region of the global optic flow field and triangulating two or more vectors. Consistent with this hypothesis, humans are capable of estimating their path to within 2° of visual angle even in extremely sparse flow fields consisting of ten dots (Warren et al., 1988).

Furthermore, the alignment of the focus of expansion with the direction of heading does not depend on the spatial structure of the environment. If it did, the moving observer would need to know whether the environmental layout satis-fied certain necessary conditions. Fortunately, this is not the case. Regardless of whether one is moving over a ground plane, toward a wall, or through a dense forest, the location of the FoE specifies heading direction. Prior knowledge of the layout of the environment, which is a challenging problem in its own right, is not necessary. Indeed, heading judgments based on optic flow are accurate regardless of whether one is traveling over a ground plane, toward a wall, or through a cloud of points (Warren et al., 1988).

One might wonder how an idea as simple and intuitive as Gibson's optic flow hypothesis could be the impetus for decades of research and draw the attention of researchers from so many fields, including not only psychological science but also neuroscience, biology, computer vision, and robotics. One reason is that the problem of perceiving heading from optic flow is not simply a matter of locating the FoE. In naturalistic environments, the presence of moving objects, the need to direct gaze toward objects of interest, and the necessity to move along paths that are more complex than a straight line alter the radial flow pattern. In the next few sections, we will examine how humans perceive self-motion direction under these less idealized but more naturalistic conditions.

2.4.2 Heading Perception in the Presence of Moving Objects

One factor that could complicate the perception of heading based on optic flow is the presence of objects that move independently of ourselves, such as pedestrians, automobiles, and cyclists. When such objects are present, as they often are, they introduce regions of the optic flow field with motion that is discrepant from that generated by the stationary background. In the instantaneous flow field, the velocity vectors corresponding to a moving object have different magnitudes and (in most cases) point in different directions.

To appreciate the challenge faced by the visual system, let us return to the cycling scenario from earlier but now imagine that you are on a road approaching an intersection and the light is green. Shortly before you enter the intersection, a car traveling along a cross street runs the red light and crosses through the intersection in front of you. Figure 2 depicts the optic flow field at the instant that the car (represented here as a rectangle for the sake of simplicity) crosses your path. Note that a large part of the visual field is taken up by optic flow from the car. Although the path of the car is perpendicular to your path, the flow vectors do not point directly sideways because your own forward self-motion brings you closer to the car, causing it to optically expand within your visual field. In fact, the flow vectors within the contours of the object radiate from a single point – a focus of expansion corresponding to flow from the object – that is in a different location than the FoE generated by the background flow and specifies one's heading relative to the moving object. For example, the object FoE's location just to the right of the object in Figure 2 specifies that the

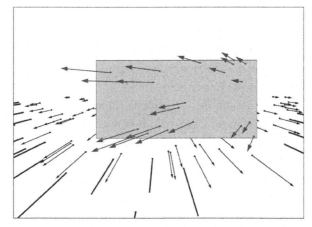

Figure 2 Optic flow field generated by forward self-motion with a moving object crossing the path from right to left. Color version of figure available at www.cambridge.org/fajen

observer is on course to pass just to the right of the object. At the same time, the background FoE and the portions of the flow field that are most informative about actual heading are occluded by the object. If heading perception was simply based on the FoE of the most dominant radial pattern, heading judgments would be dramatically biased at that instant. Yet we do not seem to experience large shifts in perceived heading whenever someone or something cuts in front of our future path. Psychophysical studies conducted in the laboratory, where perceived heading can be measured with precision, reveal that moving objects can induce biases in heading perception. However, the effect is small (on the order of a few degrees) and occurs only when the object occludes or almost occludes the background FoE (Warren & Saunders, 1995; Royden & Hildreth, 1996; Layton & Fajen, 2016c; Layton & Fajen, 2017). Thus, heading perception is surprisingly robust and stable in the presence of moving objects.

To what should we attribute this robustness and stability? One possibility is that the visual system identifies and segments moving objects prior to heading estimation. Indeed, there are numerous static and dynamic cues that the visual system could use to segment moving objects during self-motion (Raudies & Neumann, 2013). However, empirical support for the segmentation hypothesis is mixed. Dokka, Park, Jansen, DeAngelis, and Angelaki (2019) found that on trials in which the moving object was correctly detected, heading judgments were less biased compared to trials with identical stimuli in which the moving object was not detected. This suggests that optic flow from moving objects might be discounted during heading perception, at least when those objects are correctly detected as moving. On the other hand, in the majority of studies demonstrating heading biases resulting from moving objects (Warren & Saunders, 1995; Royden & Hildreth, 1996; Layton & Fajen, 2016c; Layton & Fajen, 2017), the moving object was easily identifiable based on relative motion and dynamic occlusion. Even the addition of color contrast, binocular disparity, or biological motion cues to facilitate segmentation does not reduce the bias (Li, Ni, Lappe, Niehorster, & Sun, 2018; Riddell, Li, & Lappe, 2019). This implies a spatial pooling mechanism that pools motion from across the entire visual field regardless of whether it corresponds to moving objects or the stationary background (Warren & Saunders, 1995; Layton, Mingolla, & Browning, 2012).

Another possible explanation for the robustness to moving objects is that heading perception is a process that evolves over time and is based on the temporal evolution of the optic flow field rather than a snapshot (Layton & Fajen, 2016d; Layton & Fajen, 2016b). In other words, perceived heading at the instant depicted in Figure 2 is based on not only the instantaneous flow field at that moment but also the optic flow prior to that point, before the more informative regions of the flow field were occluded by the object. Layton and Fajen (2016d) tested this hypothesis by varying how much of the earlier part of the stimulus leading up to the last frame was presented to subjects. Indeed, the heading bias was greatest when the stimulus was short in duration and included only the portion of the event in which the moving object occluded the background FoE. When stimulus duration was longer and the earlier part of the sequence prior to occlusion was included, the heading bias was reduced. Layton and Fajen (2016b) interpreted this as evidence that the neural mechanisms that detect information in optic flow are best understood as a dynamical system whose activity at any one point in time depends on the temporally evolving flow field.

2.4.3 Heading Perception during Rotation

Let us now turn to another reason why heading perception is not simply a matter of locating the FoE: most naturalistic locomotor tasks involve rotations of the eyes, head, and body that alter the global radial flow pattern generated by pure translation. Returning once again to the cycling example, imagine that you approach another intersection and wonder whether the crossing street is the one where you need to make a right turn. You notice a street sign off to the right side and shift your gaze in its direction to read the name of the road. As you continue moving forward toward the intersection, you rotate your eyes rightward to maintain fixation on the sign. Such smooth pursuit eye movements introduce motion on your retina that alters the radially expanding pattern that was projected onto your retina when you were looking straight ahead. The instantaneous retinal flow is now the vector sum of two components – a translational component (T) that results from your forward movement along a straight path and a rotational component (R) that results from rotations of the eye. You are already familiar with T and its radially expanding structure; let us consider R.

The first important thing to know about R is that pursuit eye movements generate motion in the direction opposite that of the eye movements. In the example above, the rightward eye rotations needed to maintain fixation on the sign generate leftward motion on the retina. The second thing to know is that the magnitude of flow resulting from pure rotation is proportional to the rate of eye rotation and independent of the distance to the object generating the flow. Third, the flow vectors in R are parallel; that is, they all point in the same direction. Note that these same principles apply to rotations of the head and body. Thus, the rotational component in the flow field is determined by the combined rate of rotation of the eyes in the head, the head on the body, and the body in the world.

Putting it all together in the context of the cycling example above, the rightward eye rotations needed to maintain fixation of the road sign generate uniform leftward flow on the retina. The combined retinal flow field, which also includes the component due to translation, is depicted in Figure 3A. Notably absent from the retinal flow due to T+R is the FoE. Unlike the flow field due to pure translation, there is no immediately identifiable feature in the direction of heading. Furthermore, although the actual self-motion is linear, the

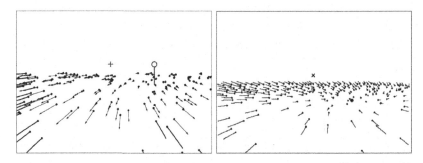

Figure 3 (A) Retinal flow field generated by forward translation with rightward smooth pursuit eye movements to maintain fixation of a point at eye level. (B) Retinal flow generated by forward translation with rightward smooth pursuit eye movements to maintain fixation of a point on the ground. Reprinted by permission from Springer Nature Customer Service Center GmbH: Springer Nature, Nature, Direction of self-motion is perceived from optical flow, William H. Warren et al., Copyright 1988.

instantaneous retinal flow field has a definite curvilinear shape to it. Nonetheless, humans do not perceive themselves to be moving along a curved path under such conditions (except when eye rotations are simulated, as in some laboratory experiments, including those discussed later in this section). In fact, observers are capable of accurately perceiving their direction of self-motion while making pursuit eye movements (Warren & Hannon, 1988).

In the example depicted in Figure 3A, the fixation point is at eye level and so the axis of rotation is vertical. Figure 3B depicts the retinal flow resulting from linear self-motion with fixation of a point on the ground (e.g., if you were looking for a landmark on the ground to determine whether this was the correct street to turn right). In this scenario, the retinal motion flows outward from a single point somewhat reminiscent of Figure 1B. However, the motion pattern has a spiral rather than a radial shape, and the singularity is located at the fixation point rather than in the direction of heading. This provides yet another reminder that heading perception is not simply about locating the singularity in the flow field. If it was, humans would confuse the direction in which they are looking with the direction in which they are heading.

The question of how moving observers perceive heading while making pursuit eye movements is sometimes called the rotation problem and has been the focus of dozens of studies. A detailed summary of this large body of work is beyond the scope of this Element. The goal here is to develop intuitions about how the visual system might solve the rotation problem and to become familiar with a few of the key studies on this topic.

Most theories of heading perception during rotation fall into one of two categories: extraretinal theories and retinal theories. The former assumes a key role for nonvisual information about the rate of eye, head, or body rotation. This could include efferent signals associated with activation of extraocular and neck muscles, proprioceptive information about eye and head rotation, and vestibular information about head rotation. Such information could be used to estimate the component of the retinal flow field that is due to rotation and needs to be subtracted out. If this process is accurate, what remains is the flow due to translation with a radial pattern that specifies heading.

Retinal theories rely entirely on information in retinal flow to recover heading and come in several varieties. For example, the retinal motion of distant elements is weakly affected by observer translation (due to motion parallax) and hence largely a consequence of observer rotation. If depth information is available to specify which regions of the flow field contain motion from distant elements, the rotational component can be estimated based on the flow from those regions and then subtracted to recover the translational component (Van den Berg & Brenner, 1994a; Van den Berg & Brenner, 1994b). Alternatively, the visual system could rely on motion parallax. Consider the retinal flow from two elements in the same visual direction at different distances. The translational components share a common direction (both vectors point away from the FoE) but differ in magnitude (the vector corresponding to the nearby element is longer). The rotational components are the same because flow due to rotation is independent of distance. Therefore, if we subtract one retinal flow vector from the other, the rotational components cancel out and what is left points directly toward or away (depending on the order of the two elements when we subtract) from the FoE. This is known as the differential motion parallax hypothesis (Longuet-Higgins & Prazdny, 1980; Rieger & Lawton, 1985).

A popular approach to testing the extraretinal and retinal accounts involves the use of a technique called simulated rotation (Regan & Beverley, 1982; Warren & Hannon, 1988). Consider once again the cycling example, but this time imagine that you are wearing a helmet mounted with a miniature video camera (e.g., a GoPro) to record the event. Suppose that your head (and therefore, the camera) is pointed 5° to the right of your direction of travel and remains at that same orientation as you approach the intersection with the road sign, which is initially 15° to the right of heading. If you were to watch the video on your computer monitor later, there would be a FoE located 5° to the left of the center of the screen and the road sign would drift rightward on the screen. If you tried to keep your eyes pointed at the road sign as you watched the video replay, you would have to actively generate pursuit eye movements and/or rotate your head. Let us call this the actual rotation video (see Video 1).

Now imagine that you repeat your ride down the same street but this time you point your head and the camera toward the road sign and rotate them as you approach the intersection to keep the head and camera pointed toward the sign. When you watch the video on your computer screen, the heading direction would drift leftward on the screen while the road sign would remain in a fixed screen position. I will refer to this as the simulated rotation video (Video 2).

Here is the key point – if you fixate the road sign while watching the two videos, the visual information will be the same, but the nonvisual information will differ. For both videos, the road sign will project onto your fovea and the heading direction will drift leftward on your retina. The retinal flow will be the same. However, to fixate the road sign in the actual rotation video, you must actively rotate your eyes and/or head, which generates efferent signals, proprioceptive information, and vestibular information. In contrast, fixating the road sign in the simulated rotation video involves keeping your eyes pointed in the same direction so the nonvisual information will specify no rotation.

The convenient thing about this situation is that the two aforementioned categories of solutions to the rotation problem (i.e., the extraretinal and the

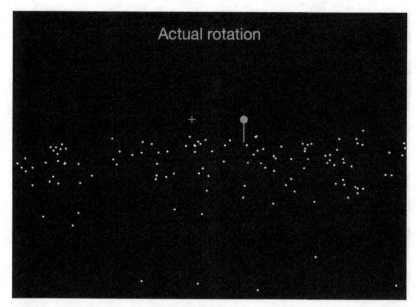

Video 1 Actual rotation condition simulating linear self-motion with camera pointed 5° to the right of the direction of travel and remaining at that orientation. The cross indicates the direction of heading (i.e., FoE). The circle and post correspond to the road sign, which is initially 15° to the right of heading but drifts to the right as the camera moves. Video available at www.cambridge.org /fajen

retinal solutions) make different predictions about the accuracy of heading judgments under these conditions. The extraretinal hypothesis relies on both visual and nonvisual information and therefore predicts that heading judgments should be accurate only when rotations of the eyes and head are real (i.e., in the actual rotation condition). In contrast, the retinal hypothesis assumes that visual information is sufficient and so predicts that heading judgments should be accurate in both cases.

Numerous studies have compared heading perception under real and simulated rotation conditions. In impoverished environments, such as when texture elements are sparse and there is minimal motion parallax, heading judgments are generally accurate when eye movements are real and biased when they are simulated (Royden, Banks, & Crowell, 1992; Royden, Crowell, & Banks, 1994). This is consistent with a role for extraretinal information. Interestingly, the biases exhibited during simulated rotation are consistent with the illusion of traveling along a curvilinear path. However, observers can accurately perceive heading in simulated rotation conditions provided that the visual environment

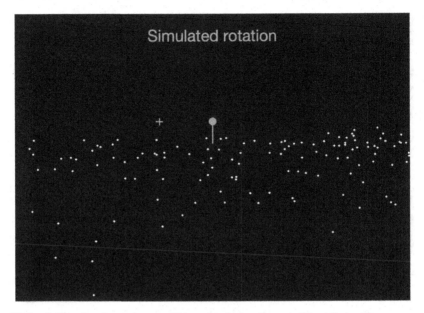

Video 2 Simulated rotation condition simulating linear self-motion with camera rotated as it moves to keep the road sign (circle and post) at a fixed position on the screen. The cross indicates the direction of heading, which drifts to the left as the camera moves. Video available at www.cambridge.org/fajen

contains dense texture and depth variation to provide sufficient motion parallax (Li & Warren, 2000). This implies that observers are capable of perceiving heading based on visual information alone and supports the differential motion parallax hypothesis. Li and Warren also pointed out that the simulated rotation condition is a cue conflict situation – extraretinal information specifies no rotation, whereas visual information specifies that the eye is rotating. Thus, the fact that heading judgments were accurate in the simulated rotation condition (provided that dense motion parallax is available) led Li and Warren to conclude that visual information dominates extraretinal information.

Before moving on from the topic of heading perception during eye movements, it is worth considering an assumption that underlies most of the research on this topic – namely, that eye movements either complicate or are transparent to the perception of heading. Over the years, a number of researchers have called this assumption into question based on evidence suggesting that eye movements may actually be part of the solution rather than part of the problem. One such account, which was proposed by Kim and Turvey (1999) and Wann and Swapp (2000; Wann & Land, 2000), is described in Section 2.4.5. More recently, researchers have used mobile eye tracking systems to record retinal flow and head-centric optic flow generated by walking in naturalistic environments. These studies reveal that oscillations of the head associated with walking cause the FoE in head-centric optic flow to jump around at high velocities within the visual field (Matthis, Muller, Bonnen, & Hayhoe, 2020). In contrast, the retinal flow, which also includes components due to eye rotation, is more stable (see also Durant & Zanker, 2020) and contains information that walkers could use to control locomotion. For example, a walker's nominal heading (left or right) relative to the fixated object is specified by the sign and magnitude of the curl at the fovea, which Matthis et al. showed was a stable and reliable feature of retinal flow. These findings raise some interesting questions about whether eye movements complicate or simplify the problem of perceiving heading from optic flow.

2.4.4 Heading Perception during Curvilinear Self-Motion

Another source of rotational flow is curvilinear self-motion, which is movement of the body along a curved path such as a bend in the road. Curvilinear self-motion differs from rotation due to eye movements in that the axis of rotation is at a distance rather than at the center of the eye.

When observers move along a straight trajectory, their instantaneous heading and future path are aligned. During curvilinear self-motion, the two diverge – instantaneous heading is the tangent to the curvilinear path, and the future path is the trajectory that the observer would follow if path curvature remains fixed. At least in principle, both could play a role in the visual guidance of locomotion, although in different ways. The ability to perceive instantaneous heading could be useful by serving as a reference axis against which the directions of goals and obstacles are measured, as assumed in some models of locomotor control (e.g., Fajen & Warren, 2003). Likewise, the ability to perceive one's future path would allow observers to determine where they will be in the future if current conditions persist, which in turn would allow them to adjust their trajectory if necessary to reach goals or avoid obstacles (Wilkie & Wann, 2006). The remainder of this section will focus on the perception of instantaneous heading. We will turn to the perception of future curvilinear path in Section 2.4.5.

The problem of perceiving instantaneous heading during curvilinear self-motion is actually the same as the problem of perceiving heading during translation with eye rotation, which we just discussed. The two problems are the same because instantaneous heading is, by definition, the direction of self-motion at any one point in time and therefore independent of whether the observer is traveling along a straight or curved path. Likewise, as mentioned above, the instantaneous flow field generated by curvilinear self-motion is formally equivalent to that generated by linear self-motion with eye rotation. As such, the same information that is used to perceive heading during translation plus rotation (i.e., the velocity vector field) could also be used to perceive instantaneous heading during curvilinear self-motion.

There is ample evidence that observers are capable of accurately perceiving instantaneous heading during curvilinear self-motion (Stone & Perrone, 1997; Li, Sweet, & Stone, 2006; Li, Chen, & Peng, 2009; Li, Stone, & Chen, 2011; Li & Cheng, 2011; but see Wilkie & Wann, 2006 for conflicting evidence). The most compelling evidence comes from studies by Li Li and colleagues in which observers adjusted the orientation of a simulated vehicle that was traveling on a circular path until it was aligned with the instantaneous heading. Heading judgments remain accurate even in the absence of information that is needed to estimate the future path, provided that depth range and field of view are sufficiently large to generate rich motion parallax (Li et al., 2009). This suggests that humans do not first perceive the future path and then recover heading by estimating the tangent (although observers may still use this strategy if motion parallax is reduced). Interestingly, observers are also capable of accurately perceiving their instantaneous heading during curvilinear self-motion in the presence of simulated eye rotation (Li & Cheng, 2011). Perrone (2018) recently introduced a computational model that estimates instantaneous heading during curvilinear movement by combining optic flow with vestibular information.

2.4.5 Perception of Future Path

It is one thing to know one's heading direction at an instant, but moving about in cluttered environments also requires the ability to anticipate where one could be in the future. In this section, I will consider one perceptual capability that could support anticipatory control – namely, the perception of one's future path. Let us define the future path as the trajectory through the world that one would follow if path curvature remains constant. On a bicycle, the ability to perceive one's future curvilinear path would allow you to see if you are on a course to safely avoid a pothole if the handlebars are kept in a fixed position. Our focus will be on scenarios involving curvilinear self-motion because during linear self-motion, future path coincides with instantaneous heading, which was discussed in Section 2.4.4.

The first step in understanding the perception of future curvilinear path is to envision the optic flow that results from curvilinear self-motion. Imagine that you are following a road that bends sharply to the right. As you move, the texture elements on the ground plane follow hyperbolic-shaped flow lines (Warren, Mestre, Blackwell, & Morris, 1991), as depicted in Figure 4.

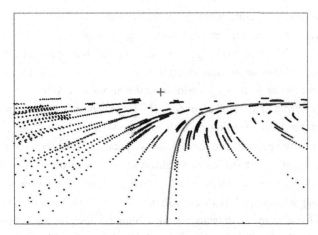

Figure 4 Flow lines generated by curvilinear self-motion over a ground plane. The solid curve corresponds to the locomotor flow line. Color version of figure available at www.cambridge.org/fajen

There are several characteristics of curvilinear flow fields that are important to know. First, one of the flow lines passes directly beneath the observer (see the solid curve in Figure 4). Lee and Lishman (1980) referred to this as the locomotor flow line and pointed out that it coincides with the path that the observer would follow, assuming path curvature remains fixed (i.e., the future path). Texture elements to the inside of the locomotor flow line reverse their horizontal direction of motion, whereas those on the outside do not. The boundary that separates reversing and nonreversing flow lines is known as the reversal boundary and also coincides with the future path (Warren et al., 1991).

The second thing to notice is the absence of a focus of expansion. During self-motion along a circular path, there is no point from which all velocity vectors radiate as there is during linear self-motion. However, the flow field generated during self-motion along a circular path does contain a singularity – the optic flow at the center of rotation of the observer's path is zero. The distance from the observer to the center of rotation is called the radius of curvature (r) and is a commonly used metric of the degree of curvature of the observer's path. The shorter the radius of curvature, the sharper the path. Relying on the distance to center of rotation to estimate path curvature is a bit more complicated than it sounds because this point is 180 degrees from the tangent to the path. As such, unless the observer is looking toward the inside of the path, the center of rotation may be in the periphery or outside the field of view. Nevertheless, the normals to any two velocity vectors intersect at the center of rotation (Warren et al., 1991), which means that there is information about the location of the center of rotation even if it falls outside the field of view.

Third, recall that the instantaneous velocity vector field is formally ambiguous in the sense that the optical motion generated by self-motion along a curvilinear path with fixed gaze is identical to that generated by some combination of translation plus rotation (i.e., linear self-motion with pursuit eye movements) as well as by various combinations of eye rotation and path curvature (Warren et al., 1991; Royden, 1994). This point has important implications for our understanding of path perception from optic flow. Although a single velocity vector field unambiguously specifies the observer's instantaneous heading, it is not sufficient to allow observers to distinguish between a continuum of possible trajectories through the world, ranging from self-motion along a linear path with eye rotation to self-motion along a curvilinear path with fixed gaze. Understanding how humans perceive their future path despite this ambiguity is one of the things that make this problem both challenging and interesting.

One possible solution is that the visual system resolves the ambiguity by detecting changes in the flow field over time. The aforementioned ambiguity applies only to the instantaneous optic flow field. In representations of the flow field that include higher-order components (i.e., acceleration or curvature), the flow fields generated by curvilinear self-motion and translation plus rotation diverge (Rieger, 1983). In particular, whereas the flow field generated by curvilinear self-motion with fixed gaze angle is stationary with constant streamlines in retinal coordinates, the flow resulting from translation plus rotation deforms (i.e., successive flow fields vary). Nevertheless, the evidence from psychophysical studies indicates that the presence of higher-order components in the flow field is neither necessary nor sufficient to accurately perceive future path during curvilinear self-motion (Warren, Blackwell, Kurtz, Hatsopoulos, & Kalish, 1991; Li & Cheng, 2011), which does not support the hypothesis that humans perceive their future path by detecting changes in the flow field over time.

Kim and Turvey (1999) and Wann and Swapp (2000) proposed another clever solution that relies on sensitivity to curvature in the retinal flow field to perceive future path. They discovered that if one maintains fixation of an object on the future path, texture elements all along the future path flow directly downwards on the retina (Figure 5). If the future path lies to the left or right of the fixated object, retinal flow lines curve rightward or leftward respectively. As such, sensitivity to curvature in the retinal flow field would allow observers to determine whether their future path lies to the left or right of the fixated object. This hypothesis predicts that judgments of future path should be accurate when observers fixate a point on or near their future path, even if eye rotations are simulated. Contrary to this prediction, Saunders and Ma (2011) found that

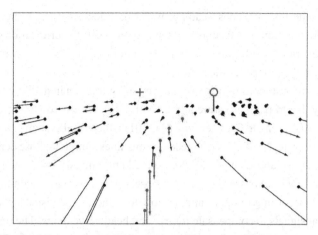

Figure 5 Retinal flow generated by moving along a curvilinear path and fixating an object at eye level that lies directly above the future path. Color version of figure available at www.cambridge.org/fajen

observers made large errors in future path judgments under such conditions. The findings of that study argue against this hypothesis (but see Wilkie & Wann, 2006) and further weaken the hypothesis that observers rely on sensitivity to acceleration or curvature in the retinal flow field to resolve ambiguity.

Another possibility is that observers could estimate path curvature by tracking changes in heading over time. Formally, path curvature (κ) is equal to the ratio of the rate of change of instantaneous heading (R) to tangential speed of self-motion (T) (i.e., $\kappa = R/T$). Thus, if observers could perceive the change in heading and if they know their self-motion speed, they could estimate path curvature. What makes this hypothesis appealing is that the instantaneous velocity vector field is sufficient to estimate heading even during eye rotation or curvilinear self-motion. Thus, it offers a possible answer to the question of how humans perceive future path despite their insensitivity to higher-order components of the flow field. However, the data do not support this hypothesis either (Saunders, 2010; Saunders & Ma, 2011; Li & Cheng, 2011; Cheng & Li, 2012).

The hypothesis with the strongest empirical support is that humans rely on rotation in the instantaneous flow field to perceive their future curvilinear path (Banks, Ehrlich, Backus, & Crowell, 1996; Saunders, 2010; Saunders & Ma, 2011; Li & Cheng, 2011; Cheng & Li, 2012). This hypothesis, which I will refer to as the rotational flow hypothesis, makes two important assumptions. The first is that extraretinal signals about eye and head rotation are available and that the visual system uses such information to compensate for any rotational flow resulting from such movements. The second is that the body does not rotate relative to the instantaneous heading, which is often the case during natural forms of locomotion. For example, when driving a car, the orientation of one's body is generally fixed relative to the orientation of the car, which in turn is aligned with the tangent to the path.

If these two assumptions are met, the remaining rotation in the flow field will be entirely due to path curvature and the velocity vector field will be constant over time. According to Saunders and Ma (2011), the visual system extrapolates the visual trajectories of objects to recover flow lines similar to those depicted in Figure 4. As Lee and Lishman (1980) pointed out, one of those flow lines (the locomotor flow line) passes beneath the observer and coincides with the future path. Thus, according to the rotational flow hypothesis, the visual system uses extraretinal signals to compensate for eye and head movements. The remaining flow field is constant over time and can therefore be used to recover flow lines from which the future path can be estimated. (See Li & Cheng, 2011; Cheng & Li, 2012 for an alternative account that also relies on rotational flow.) This hypothesis accounts for the fact that future path judgments are accurate when the orientation of the body is fixed relative to instantaneous heading (Saunders, 2010; Cheng & Li, 2012) but inaccurate when the orientation of the body changes relative to instantaneous heading (Cheng & Li, 2010; Cheng & Li, 2012; Li & Cheng, 2011; Saunders, 2010; Saunders & Ma, 2011).

2.5 Perception of Object Motion during Self-Motion (Flow Parsing)

In Section 2.4.2, I discussed the perception of heading in the presence of moving objects. For many tasks, it is also necessary to perceive how the object itself is moving. To appreciate the problem, consider Figure 6A, which depicts the optic flow field generated when an observer moves straight ahead, while a moving object (in this case, a single red dot) moves from right to left across the observer's future path. The motion of the dot in the optic array reflects the relative motion between the observer and the object. The flow field in Figure 6A can be separated into two components – one that reflects the motion of the observer, assuming the object is stationary (Figure 6B), and another that reflects the motion of the object, assuming the observer is stationary (Figure 6C). Thus, the optic flow field depicted in Figure 6A is the vector sum of the self-motion component and the object motion component. To perceive the motion of the object in a world-centered reference frame, the visual system must somehow factor out the influence of self-motion, which is known as flow parsing (Warren & Rushton, 2007). The component that remains is that which is due to object motion alone, independent of the observer's self-motion.

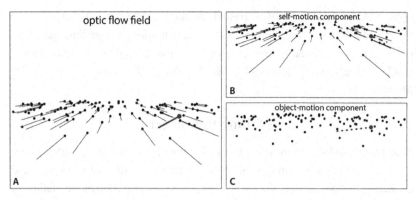

Figure 6 Decomposition of optic flow field into self-motion and object motion
components. (A) Optic flow field generated by self-motion with an object
(larger dot) moving from right to left. (B and C) Component of optic flow field
due to self-motion and object motion. Figure 1 from Fajen & Matthis (2013)
adapted with color changes licensed under CC BY. Color version of figure
available at www.cambridge.org/fajen

Based on Figure 6, it would seem that the visual system first estimates
heading and then uses that estimate to parse the flow field. However, there is
evidence that object motion estimates can be more precise than heading judgments and that certain manipulations that affect the accuracy of heading judgments have no effect on the accuracy of object motion judgments (Rushton,
Chen, & Li, 2018; Warren, Rushton, & Foulkes, 2012). This suggests that
heading perception and object motion perception rely on common mechanisms
at an early stage but may involve independent mechanisms at a later stage.

It would also seem that flow parsing is simply a matter of detecting the
background flow in the neighborhood of the moving object and subtracting
that flow from the local motion of the object. However, flow parsing is not
merely the result of local motion subtraction. Even when the background flow
surrounding the object is masked, observers are capable of parsing the flow
field (Warren & Rushton, 2009b), suggesting a global discounting of optic
flow. Furthermore, the component of the object's optical motion that is due to
self-motion (i.e., the component that must be factored out) depends on how far
away the object is. Thus, to correctly parse the optic flow field and accurately
perceive the motion of the object, information about the depth of the object or
the object's location within the 3D optic flow field must be available. Indeed,
when depth information is unavailable or when observers misperceive the
depth of the object, the accuracy of flow parsing degrades (Warren & Rushton,
2007; Warren & Rushton, 2009a). Lastly, although self-motion is specified by

optic flow, manipulations of nonvisual self-motion information also influence the perception of object motion during self-motion, suggesting that flow parsing is an inherently multisensory process (Fajen & Matthis, 2013; Dokka, MacNeilage, DeAngelis, & Angelaki, 2013; Fajen, Parade, & Matthis, 2013).

2.6 Time-to-Contact

In addition to informing moving observers about their direction of heading, optic flow also contains information about one's proximity relative to objects and surfaces. However, unlike the static depth cues that are available to stationary observers and specify only spatial proximity, optic flow also contains information about one's temporal proximity; that is, the amount of time remaining until the observer makes contact with the thing toward which they are moving. Depending on the observer's goal, such information could be useful for purposes of dodging an obstacle, initiating movements to capture a target, or bracing for impact.

In terms of spatial variables, the time remaining until contact (or time-to-contact, TTC) with an approached object or opening, assuming constant velocity, is equal to the distance (d) to the object divided by the approach speed (v). However, neither distance nor approach speed need to be estimated to perceive TTC. For TTC can also be expressed in terms of optical variables that are immediately available to a moving observer; namely, the size of the optical angle (θ) subtended by the approach object and the rate of change of θ (i.e., $\dot{\theta}$) (Figure 7A). As the observer moves toward the object, both θ and $\dot{\theta}$ increase (a phenomenon known as looming) (Figure 7B). However, the ratio of θ to its rate of change $\dot{\theta}$ approximates the amount of time remaining until the observer collides with the object (Lee 1974, 1976, 1980). This ratio ($\theta/\dot{\theta}$) is known as the optical variable tau (τ). Thus, TTC $\approx \tau = \theta/\dot{\theta}$.

Although θ depends on the size of the approached object and $\dot{\theta}$ depends on both object size and approach speed, the ratio of θ to $\dot{\theta}$ specifies TTC independently of size and approach speed. It is for this reason that τ is sometimes referred to as an optical invariant; its relation to TTC is invariant over changes in object size and approach speed. As such, the moving observer does not need to know the size or distance of the approach object or the speed of self-motion. τ allows the observer to directly perceive TTC.

Other τ-like variables specify the moving observer's temporal relation to the environment. When the moving observer is on course to pass by the object rather than collide with it, the amount of time remaining until passage (or time-to-passage, TTP) is optically specified by the ratio of the angular position of the object relative to the direction of heading to its rate of change (Kaiser &

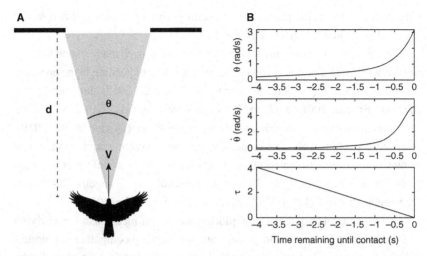

Figure 7 (A) Top-down view of a bird approaching an opening. d, v, and θ are the distance, approach speed, and visual angle of the opening, respectively. (B) Time series of θ, $\dot{\theta}$, and τ, illustrating that τ closely approximates the amount of time remaining until contact with the opening.

Mowafy, 1993). This variable is dubbed global tau to distinguish it from so-called local tau described in the previous paragraphs.

2.7 Neural Mechanisms and Neural Modeling

One of the exciting aspects of conducting research on the perception of self-motion and object motion from optic flow is the synergy that exists between behavioral, neurophysiological, and computational approaches. Indeed, many of the same questions about the perception of self-motion, object motion, or time-to-contact that have been addressed using psychophysical and behavioral methods (as described above) can also be approached from a neurophysiological or computational perspective. In many cases, these studies have provided converging evidence (Warren, 2004) or led to new hypotheses and solutions.

The first discoveries of areas of the primate brain that respond to optic flow patterns were made in the 1980s and 1990s. These studies revealed cells in the dorsal region of the medial superior temporal area (MSTd) of the macaque visual cortex with large receptive fields and selectivity for the kinds of optic flow patterns that are generated by self-motion (e.g., radial, laminar, rotational, and spiral flow) (Saito et al., 1986; Tanaka & Saito, 1989; Duffy & Wurtz, 1991; Graziano, Andersen, & Snowden, 1994). Judgments of heading can be biased by microstimulation of MSTd cells in monkeys, providing evidence that MST plays a direct role in the perception of heading from optic flow (Britten & van Wezel, 1998; Gu, Deangelis, & Angelaki, 2012).

Over the past 15 years, a great deal of progress has been made in understanding the neural mechanisms involved in the perception of heading in the presence of moving objects (Dokka, DeAngelis, & Angelaki, 2015) and during eye rotation (Britten, 2008; Sunkara, DeAngelis, & Angelaki, 2016), as well as the perception of object motion during self-motion (Dokka et al., 2019). Interestingly, MSTd cells also respond to vestibular system activity and appear to play a key role in the integration of visual and vestibular information about self-motion (Greenlee et al., 2016; Gu, Angelaki, & Deangelis, 2008; Gu, DeAngelis, & Angelaki, 2007; Angelaki, Gu, & Deangelis, 2011).

Another valuable approach to exploring the neural mechanisms underlying self-motion and object motion perception is to develop computational models (Elder, Grossberg, & Mingolla, 2009; Lappe et al., 1999; Layton & Fajen, 2016a; Perrone, 1992). These models comprise units that respond and are organized in a way that is similar to cells found in areas of the brain that are involved in the processing of optic flow (e.g., MT, MST). Modeling has proven to be a useful approach to both unifying findings from the large body of literature on optic flow and exploring possible mechanisms through simulation, which in turn can generate novel predictions that then drive further experiments. Such models have also been adapted for use in ground-based and aerial robotic systems that rely on vision to guide navigation (Escobar-Alvarez et al., 2017).

3 Perception of Spatial Layout and Affordances by an Active Observer

In addition to perceiving their movement and proximity relative to things in the environment, moving observers also need to perceive the spatial layout of surfaces and objects in order to control action. Most readers will be familiar with the study of visual depth perception and the multitude of visual depth cues (e.g., accommodation, convergence, height in the visual field, and familiar size) that enable us to perceive the three-dimensional structure of the environment. Indeed, 3D depth perception is among the most commonly covered topics in introductory psychology courses and among the oldest and most extensively studied in the field of vision science.

In this section, we will situate the problem of spatial layout perception in the context of an active observer existing in a natural environment engaged in some natural locomotor task. When we adopt this perspective, it becomes clear that the perception of spatial layout is fundamentally embodied and deeply intertwined with the control of action. As we will see, to be immediately useful for the purposes of guiding locomotion, the relevant dimensions of the environment could be perceived in relation to dimensions and action capabilities of the body. For example, by perceiving the height of a large tree that has fallen onto a hiking path as a proportion of their leg length, a hiker could immediately see whether the tree can be stepped over or must be circumvented. This is a radical idea because we are so accustomed to measuring dimensions of the world in units like inches, feet, and meters that are independent of the person doing the measuring (i.e., extrinsic units). The novel insight here is that our perceptions of the dimensions of the world are in intrinsic units that are defined by the dimensions of the perceiver. We begin with an analysis of the visual information that makes it possible for observers to perceive spatial layout in intrinsic units.

3.1 Body-Scaled and Action-Scaled Information

Imagine standing on a walking path in a park facing a lamppost (see Figure 8). γ_{A+B} is the visual angle subtended by the lamppost from its base on the ground to its top and can be divided into two smaller visual angles (γ_A and γ_B) at the point on the lamppost at the level of the observer's eye. If the ground is flat and the horizon is visible in the distance, it cuts the lamppost at a height equal to eye level. Even if the horizon is not visible, information about eye level is available from convergence of parallel edges (e.g., road edges), the gravitational horizontal, and (if the observer is moving parallel to the ground) the height of the FoE.

The ratio of γ_{A+B} to γ_B is known as the horizon ratio (Gibson, 1979; Sedgwick, 1980) and it optically specifies the height of the lamppost (h) as a proportion of the observer's eye height (E); that is, $h/E = \gamma_{A+B}/\gamma_B$. By detecting

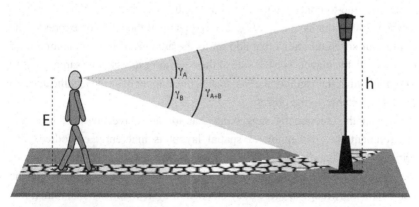

Figure 8 Diagram illustrating concept of eye-height-scaled information.

this information, the observer can perceive a dimension of the world (lamppost height) in units that are defined by a dimension of the body (eye height).

The horizon ratio is a classic example of the concept of body-scaled information. It is the availability of such information (along with action-scaled information, which is discussed below) that makes it possible for observers to perceive spatial layout in intrinsic units. Importantly, this scaling of dimensions of the environment in intrinsic units does not rely on knowledge of eye height stored in the observer's memory; such knowledge is superfluous because the information about lamppost height in the optic array is given in eye-height-scaled units. All that is needed is to detect such information. Empirical evidence exists that shows just that – when information about eye level is manipulated, the perceived size of objects is affected (Dixon, Wraga, Proffitt, & Williams, 2000; Wraga, 1999b; Wraga, 1999a).

Let us now explore how this account generalizes to dimensions other than vertical extents, leading to the idea that the entire visual scene is perceived in intrinsic units. Horizontal extents perpendicular to the line of sight such as the space between two lampposts are optically specified in eye-height-scaled units by $[2\tan(\alpha/2)]/\tan\gamma_B$, where α is the visual angle subtended by the inside edges of the two lampposts (Warren & Whang, 1987). Extents that are oriented in depth, such as the egocentric distance to a curb, are specified in units of eye height by $1/\tan\gamma_B$.

For a locomoting observer, the most immediately relevant metrics for depth extents are those that are defined not by the observer's body dimensions but rather by variables of the action system. Information that specifies dimensions in relation to units of the action system is known as action-scaled information. One such metric is stride length (L). For an walking observer, the egocentric distance (z) to an object such as a curb at the edge of a sidewalk is optically specified in units of stride length (L) by the ratio τ/T_S, where τ is the optically specified time-to-contact with the object and T_S is stride duration (see also Warren, 2007); that is $z/L = \tau/T_S$. The right side of the equation expresses the number of stride durations that add up to the amount of time remaining until contact with the object. The left side of the equation expresses the same quantity in spatial rather than temporal units; that is, the number of stride lengths that add up to the distance to the object.

I began this section by suggesting that for an active observer in a real environment, the perception of spatial layout is inherently embodied. The critical idea is that dimensions of the environment are scaled to dimensions of the observer's body and action system. What makes this possible is not the observer's knowledge of these body and action-system dimensions; rather, it is the fact that the available optical information is lawfully structured by certain characteristics of the observer, such as eye height and stride length. As such, when a parent and a small child walking along a trail encounter a stream, differences in their eye height and stride length structure the visual information available to each of them in different ways. This is why our perception of the environment is scaled to the dimensions of our body and action system and why the same region of terrain (e.g., the stream) can be seen differently in terms of its scale by observers whose bodies and action systems are different.

3.2 Affordances

The previous section builds upon conventional accounts of visual space perception by explaining how observers can perceive spatial layout in intrinsic units using body-scaled and action-scaled information. Up to this point, however, we have assumed that the objects of perception for an active observer are the geometric properties that are typically used to describe the environment, such as distances, sizes, surface orientations, and shapes. In this section, we will explore the idea that the objects of perception for an active observer are the opportunities and possibilities for action offered by the environment, or what Gibson (1979; 1977; 1966) called affordances.

A useful point of entry for understanding the theory of affordances is Figure 9, which offers a somewhat unconventional take on the kinds of properties that animals must perceive to move about. Rather than perceiving the size of the space between blades of grass, the dragonfly perceives whether it affords safe passage. Rather than perceiving the identity and 3D trajectory of motion of the flying insect, the dragonfly perceives whether it is catchable. According to the theory of affordances, these are the kinds of properties that must be perceived to successfully move around in cluttered environments.

Take a moment to consider the environments that you often inhabit and what an affordance-based description of those environments would entail. Notice the spaces between barriers or under overhangs that may (or may not) afford safe passage, the gaps between ground surfaces that may (or may not) afford crossing, the hills that may (or may not) afford ascent or descent. Consider the affordances that you encounter as a pedestrian or driver in a crowded city, a cyclist on a mountain biking trail, or an athlete on the playing field. Appreciate that some affordances, such as the passability of a gap between two moving cars, change over time or come in and out of existence as events unfold across different time scales.

An environment described in terms of affordances is parsed into categories (e.g., leap-able or not leap-able) rather than merely measured along a continuum (e.g., so many units of distance high) as is customary in descriptions of spatial

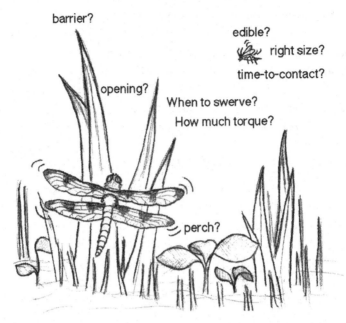

barrier?

edible?

right size?

time-to-contact?

opening?

When to swerve?

How much torque?

perch?

Figure 9 Depiction of environment in terms of action-relevant properties.
Reprinted from Figure 12.3 of Turvey & Shaw (1995).

layout (Michaels, Prindle, & Turvey, 1985; Fajen & Turvey, 2003). The bound-
aries of these categories, which are defined by the body dimensions and action
capabilities of the observer, correspond to distinct modes of behavior (Warren,
1988), such as leaping over a fallen branch on a hiking trail versus taking
a detour. In this regard, the perception of affordances provides the basis for
action selection; that is, for choosing one mode of action rather than another.

3.2.1 Perception of Affordances

Perhaps the most basic question that one can ask about affordance perception is
whether observers can reliably perceive them; that is, whether observers can
perceptually discriminate between possible and impossible actions. In a seminal
study, Warren (1984) derived a prediction from a biomechanical analysis about
the height at which stairs become unclimbable: regardless of the person's
height, stairs should be climbable up to the point at which the height of the
riser exceeds the critical value of 0.88 times the length of the person's legs. He
tested this prediction by showing observers of different statures (some taller
than average, some shorter than average) pictures of stairs of various heights
and asking them to judge whether the stairs looked climbable. Judgments were
remarkably consistent with the predictions of the biomechanical model. In

a follow-up experiment in the same study, Warren showed that observers' judgments of their preferred stair height were consistent with the heights of stairs that were energetically optimal.

Another set of questions about affordance perception concerns differences between individual perceivers with different body dimensions and action capabilities. One of the key characteristics of affordances is that they are relational. Whether a given action is possible depends on the fit between the behaviorally relevant properties of the environment and properties of actor's body and action system (e.g., stair height in relation to leg length). This implies that the proper metrics for describing the environment are intrinsic (e.g., body-scaled or action-scaled) rather than extrinsic. Consistent with this view, judgments of climbability by the two groups of subjects (tall and short) in Warren (1984) were dramatically different when stair height was measured in extrinsic units (i.e., inches) but were nearly identical when expressed in intrinsic units (i.e., leg length). In a follow-up study, Warren and Whang (1987) demonstrated an analogous effect for the perception of passability of a doorway-like aperture – subjects with wide and narrow shoulders made dramatically different judgments of passability when aperture width was expressed in extrinsic units but very similar judgments when shoulder width (an intrinsic unit) was the metric.

This pattern of findings can be understood in terms of attunement to body-scaled visual information about size. Recall that the size of a horizontal extent such as an aperture is specified in units of eye height by $[2\tan(\alpha/2)]/\tan\gamma_B$, where α is the visual angle subtended by the edges of the aperture and γ_B is the declination angle of the base of the aperture. To test whether observers rely on such information to perceive aperture passability, Warren and Whang (1987) surreptitiously manipulated eye height using a false floor, which changes the optically specified size of the aperture. Indeed, slightly elevating the floor on which the aperture walls rested above the surface on which subjects stood led to a bias to perceive apertures as larger (i.e., more passable) than they actually were.

Attunement to eye-height-scaled information explains how observers of different heights perceive aperture width in relation to eye height. To perceive whether an opening is passable, however, they need to perceive its size in relation to shoulder width. Warren and Whang (1987) argued that because shoulder width is a fixed, stable proportion of eye height when the observer is standing upright, the relation between these two units (eye height and shoulder width) can be learned through experience (a process that has come to be known as calibration; van Andel, Cole, & Pepping, 2017; Rieser, Pick, Ashmead, & Garing, 1995; Fajen, 2005b and Section 3.2.3). Thus, for a properly calibrated observer, the size of the opening can be perceived in relation to shoulder width, allowing the observer to directly perceive whether the space is wide enough to pass through.

Eye height is not the only yardstick by which sizes and distances are optically specified. If the observer is in motion, dimensions of the world are also specified in units related to the observer's movement, such as stride length and the amplitude of head sway (Fath & Fajen, 2011; Lee, 1980; Warren, 2007). Although the observer must be moving for such information to be available, neither source of information requires that the objects or surfaces that define the edges of the aperture be in contact with the ground plane. This is fortunate because many animals need to perceive the size and passability of openings, such as spaces between overhanging branches, when they are flying or swimming instead of walking on the ground.

3.2.2 Affordances Defined by Action Capabilities

Up to this point, we have focused on geometric relations between the actor and environment as the primary determinant of whether a particular action is possible. In many cases, however, affordances are dependent not only on the dimensions of the actor's body but also kinematic and kinetic characteristics (e.g., force production capabilities, locomotor speed and acceleration capabilities, flexibility). Reconsidering the affordance of stair climbability through this lens, Konzcak, Meeuwsen, and Cress (1992) demonstrated that the boundary between climbable and unclimbable can be more accurately predicted by a model that takes into account not only leg length but also leg strength and joint flexibility.

Affordances that are defined by characteristics of the observer's action system are sometimes referred to as action-scaled affordances. As with body-scaled affordances, the perception of action-scaled affordances plays an important role in decisions that actors make as they move about in complex, dynamic environments. When a pedestrian wants to cross a busy street without a stoplight, they must be able to perceive whether it is within their locomotor capabilities to reach the sidewalk on the other side of the road before the approaching cars arrive (Oudejans, Michaels, van Dort, & Frissen, 1996; Plumert & Kearney, 2014). If not, they may choose to wait or look for a crosswalk. When an animal suddenly darts onto the road in front of a moving car, the driver must be able to perceive whether it is within their car's braking capabilities to decelerate to a stop before colliding (Fajen, 2005a; Fajen, 2005c). If not, they may choose to swerve out of the way instead. When a weak fly ball is hit to short centerfield, the outfielder must perceive whether it is within their locomotor capabilities to catch the ball before it hits the ground

(Fajen, Diaz, & Cramer, 2011; Oudejans, Michaels, Bakker, & Dolné, 1996; Postma, Lemmink, & Zaal, 2018; Postma, Smith, Pepping, van Andel, & Zaal, 2017). If not, they may signal for another player to go after the ball.

Such affordances are defined by the limits of one's action capabilities. For example, whether a fly ball is catchable depends on how fast the outfielder can run. It follows that when observers perceive action-scaled affordances, they must do so in a way that somehow takes their action capabilities into account. Of course, this does not mean that actors rely on explicit knowledge of their action capabilities. Whether an outfielder is consciously aware of the fastest speed at which they can sprint is irrelevant to how accurately they can perceive whether a fly ball is catchable. So how do observers perceive affordances in a way that takes action capabilities into account?

One hypothesis is that actors "determine their capabilities anew each time they perform an action ... by picking up information about their capabilities ... that is revealed by their own actions" (Oudejans et al., 1996). This is an appealing solution, especially for those who eschew accounts of perception that rely on stored knowledge. Unfortunately, it also fails to explain how observers are able to perceive affordances before they initiate movement. It seems intuitively obvious that humans must be able to perceive the actions that are within and beyond their locomotor capabilities even while standing still. Otherwise, one would have to start crossing the street to just determine whether it is possible to reach the other side before the oncoming traffic arrives. Clearly, by the time one is in the street, it may be too late to perceive that crossing the street is not within one's capabilities. Indeed, when this hypothesis was put to the test, it was found that humans are capable of perceiving action-scaled affordances with equal accuracy regardless of whether they were stationary or moving (Fajen et al., 2011; see also Postma et al., 2018; Postma et al., 2017).

An alternative account posits a central role for calibration in the perception of action-scaled affordances (Fajen, 2005b). By this account, the relationship between the relevant intrinsic units on the perception side and the relevant intrinsic units on the action side are learned through experience. Once the mapping between units is learned, the needed action can be perceived in relation to the observer's capabilities. Just as the horizontal size of an aperture can be perceived in units of body width, the locomotor speed needed to safely cross a busy street can be perceived in units of one's maximum possible locomotor speed (Fajen & Matthis, 2011). If the minimum required speed is 40 percent of maximum possible speed, the road affords crossing; if the minimum required speed is 110 percent of maximum possible speed, the road is not crossable.

Of course, our locomotor capabilities are continually changing. As such, calibration is best understood as an ongoing process of learning. In Section 3.2.3, we consider how the perception of affordances adapts following changes in body dimensions and action capabilities.

3.2.3 Role of Exploration and Movement

Fans of the movie *Avatar* might recall the scene in which the main character Jake first awakens in his new body, which is similar in structure to a human body but is almost twice the height with long, lean limbs and torso. Initially, Jake struggles to maintain balance as he clumsily takes his first steps. His arms and tail flail uncontrollably and collide with nearby objects, as if he has no sense of his new body's dimensions. Within less than a minute, he regains the ability to not only walk and run but also perceive what he is now capable of doing; that is, he quickly learns to perceive what the world affords for his new body.

Although *Avatar* is a science fiction film, the kinds of changes to which Jake must adapt and the things he does to learn his new affordances are not entirely distinct from those that humans and other animals experience. During the first two years of life, infants experience dramatic changes in body weight, height, and motor proficiency (Adolph, 2008b; Adolph, 2008a). Their balance and coordination improve, motor variability decreases, and new modes of locomotion (e.g., crawling, cruising, walking) emerge. These changes are accompanied by dramatic changes in the child's affordances. Actions that were once impossible may now be possible (and vice versa). Even during adulthood, we experience changes that alter our affordances. Some of these are more gradual, such as those that result from strength and endurance training, pregnancy, and aging; others occur more rapidly, such as when sustaining an injury, becoming fatigued, or swapping a pair of heavy, bulky ski boots for lightweight slippers.

How does the perception of affordances adapt to such changes in body dimensions and action capabilities? What does an observer whose body has recently changed need to do to learn which actions are now within and beyond their capabilities? One seemingly logical way to answer these questions is that humans learn their new affordances through practice. For example, through trial and error, one could learn that slopes with perceived slants that are shallower than a certain value afford safe descent while slopes with steeper perceived slants afford falling. Interestingly, the evidence from numerous studies on the role of learning in affordance perception suggests otherwise; that is, practice is neither necessary nor sufficient to drive adaptation. One of the more compelling examples of the insufficiency of practice comes from studies of affordance perception in infants who have recently learned a new posture (e.g., sitting) or a new mode of locomotion (e.g., crawling) (Adolph, 2008b; Adolph, 2008a). When inexperienced infant sitters and crawlers are faced with a motor decision such as whether to cross a gap between two surfaces of support or whether to descend a ramp, they overestimate their capabilities; for example, they attempt gaps that they are unable to cross and ramps that they are unable to descend, often falling briefly before being caught by their caregivers. Interestingly, they make these kinds of errors repeatedly within a given session, despite the aversive consequences of failure. The insufficiency of practice for enabling observers to retune their perception of affordances has also been observed in adults (Mark, Balliett, Craver, Douglas, & Fox, 1990; Stoffregen, Yang, Giveans, Flanagan, & Bardy, 2009).

If learning is not driven by practice, then what do observers need to do to adapt when their body dimensions and action capabilities are altered? The answer is to do what *Avatar*'s Jake does with great enthusiasm when he first awakens in his new body – he moves, a lot! When an observer whose body has recently changed engages in activity, they reveal information about their new action capabilities and affordances. The sufficiency of active exploration was demonstrated by Mark, Baillett, Craver, Douglas, and Fox (1990), who strapped 10 cm blocks to the bottoms of subjects' shoes to alter the range of surface heights that afforded sitting. Subjects initially underestimated their action capabilities but quickly adapted to the point where they could accurately discriminate between surfaces that were and were not sit-on-able (see also, Mark, 1987). Importantly, adaptation only occurred when subjects were given an opportunity to actively move by walking, leaning their body, or rotating their head, even when such movements did not involve practice on the task of sitting. When movement was restricted, subjects were unable to recalibrate.

The ability to learn through active exploration about one's ever-changing action capabilities begins during infancy (Adolph, 2008b; Adolph, 2008a). Shortly after infants acquire a new mode of locomotion (e.g., walking), they also begin to learn exploratory behaviors specific to that mode of locomotion that allow them to adapt to changes in their bodies. Recall that infants who are inexperienced crawlers or walkers often overestimate their capabilities. When infants who are experienced in that mode of locomotion are faced with the same challenges (e.g., gaps, ramps), their motor decisions are accurately gauged to their motor capabilities. Remarkably, such decisions are accurate even if their bodies were altered in a novel way (e.g., by having them wear a weighted vest that alters their center of gravity). According to Adolph, what makes it possible for these infants to accurately perceive their affordances and rapidly adapt to novel changes is the execution of exploratory behaviors that were learned during the tens of thousands of steps per day that infants take during normal, everyday experience moving around the world.

Readers who are interested in learning more about the theory of affordances should check out the review paper by Basingerhorn et al. (2012). For those who want to learn about applications of affordance theory, I recommend Fajen, Riley, and Turvey (2008, for applications to sports), Hsu (2019, for applications to robotics), and the research of Sarah Creem-Regehr (e.g., Creem-Regehr, Stefanucci, & Thompson, 2015) for applications to virtual reality.

4 Strategies for Online Visual Control

In addition to selecting a particular action or choosing an affordance to realize, actors must also move themselves to the goal. This encompasses a broad range of behaviors from short-duration tasks that are often under ballistic control such as leaping across a gap to long-duration, large-scale navigation tasks that rely on spatial knowledge such as walking across campus from a classroom to a coffee shop. The focus of this section is on tasks that fall near the middle of this continuum – tasks that typically unfold over a period of seconds, are directed toward objects that lie within the visual field, and for which locomotion is guided based on currently available information.

4.1 Laws of Control

The importance of vision in the guidance of locomotion in humans and many other animals is uncontroversial. There is less agreement about how visual information is used to guide locomotion. One way to characterize the online visual guidance of locomotion is grounded in distinctive patterns of optic flow that observers generate by moving in a particular goal-directed manner. Gibson's (1950) strategy that involves aligning the focus of expansion with the goal (described in Section 2.3) is exemplary of this type of approach. The strategy works because the focus of expansion corresponds to the observer's direction of heading. As such, the pattern of optic flow that the observer needs to enact to achieve the task is one in which there is alignment of the FOE with the doorway opening.

Gibson (1958) was the first to describe visual guidance in such terms. He referred to such strategies as formulae, although the more commonly used terms in the current literature are control laws and control strategies (Warren, 1988; Warren, 1998b). Control laws have been proposed for a wide variety of tasks. In addition to the abovementioned strategy for steering toward a goal, there are control laws for braking to avoid a collision with an object in the path of motion (Yilmaz & Warren, 1995; Lee, 1976), intercepting moving targets that move along the ground or fly through the air (Michaels & Oudejans, 1992; Chapman, 1968), and guiding foot placement when walking or running over complex terrain (Warren, Young, & Lee, 1986; Lee, Lishman, & Thomson, 1982), just to name a few. Some of these strategies are described in more detail below.

Although each control law is unique, many of them share some important characteristics. First, control laws characterize online visual guidance as an information-based process (Warren, 1998b; Zhao & Warren, 2015). That is, the actor's behavior is primarily determined by currently available perceptual information that specifies what to do next. This contrasts with the model-based account (Loomis & Beall, 2004; see Section 5), according to which perceptual information and prior knowledge are used to construct and update internal representations or models of the environment, which in turn serve as the basis for control.

Second, in many control laws, the information upon which actors rely is task-specific in the sense that it specifies how the actor should move to perform the specific task in which he or she is engaged. This is an interesting and counterintuitive hypothesis. It challenges the common assumption that locomotion must be guided by information about the three-dimensional spatial layout of the environment, such as distances to and sizes of objects, orientations of surfaces, and so forth. Such information can be considered general-purpose because (at least, in principle) it could be repurposed for multiple tasks. According to the hypothesis under consideration here, the perception of 3D layout may be superfluous for certain tasks because everything that the actor needs to know about how to move is specified in the available task-specific information. For example, one of the most basic information-based control strategies is the constant bearing angle strategy for intercepting a moving target. This strategy will be unpacked in more detail below. For now, the important point is simply that the change in the bearing angle does not tell the actor anything about how fast the target is moving or how far away it is. Such knowledge arguably is unnecessary because the change in bearing angle already specifies how to change speed and direction to intercept the target.

Third, behavior is emergent rather than planned in advance. Actors do not follow a predetermined trajectory; rather, the trajectory emerges in real time as locomotion is regulated based on currently available information.

4.2 Current-Future Control Strategies

Let us now see how these ideas have been put to work to explain how humans use visual information to guide locomotion while performing specific locomotor tasks. As you will see, there is a common assumption shared by many information-based models about what actors perceive when engaged in such tasks. Based on what I have just covered, it should come as no surprise that the perceived properties assumed in these models are not those that describe the 3D spatial layout but rather those that are immediately relevant to the actions that the observer should perform. In this section, I will focus on models that rely on the perception of a particular kind of action-relevant property that Reinoud Bootsma (2009) cleverly dubbed the current future. The current future is a property of the actor-environment system that refers to what will happen in the future if current conditions persist. For example, in the context of a locomotor interception task, the current future refers to whether the pursuer will intercept the target, pass in front, or pass behind assuming that the pursuer's current speed and direction of locomotion remain constant. In the context of a braking task, the current future refers to whether the driver will come to a stop before, at, or after reaching the intended target location (e.g., a stop sign or mark on the road) assuming that the car's current rate of deceleration remains constant.

Characterizing visual guidance in such terms was an important development because it set the agenda for researchers. The challenge was to analyze the optic flow field to identify variables that specify the actor's current future and conduct experiments to test whether humans actually use these variables to guide locomotion. As I demonstrate in the next section, this challenge was met for several fundamental locomotor tasks.

4.2.1 Locomotor Interception of Ground-Based Moving Targets

Figure 10 depicts a current-future strategy for regulating the speed or direction of locomotion to intercept a target moving in a plane, such as along the ground plane. Locomotor interception is common in many sports (e.g., when chasing the ball carrier) and predator–prey scenarios. The particular strategy illustrated here is known as the constant bearing angle strategy because to intercept the target, the observer must move so as to keep the bearing angle of the target constant. The bearing angle is the visual angle of the moving target relative to a reference direction that remains fixed in world coordinates. This could be a distant visual landmark, such as a tall tree or mountain peak off in the distance. If the bearing angle is shrinking, the observer is moving too slowly, and the target will pass in front of them if they maintain their current speed and direction; if the bearing angle is growing, the observer is moving too quickly and the target will pass behind them if they maintain their current speed and direction. In this sense, the change in the bearing angle specifies what will happen in the future (the target will pass in front or the target will pass behind) if current conditions persist (the observer maintains current speed and direction). We can also now appreciate the sense in which the current future is an action-relevant property – it immediately

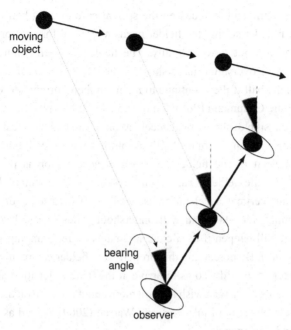

Figure 10 Observer intercepting a moving object using the constant bearing
angle strategy. Figure 1 of Fajen (2013) licensed under CC BY 3.0.

informs the observer how to modulate locomotion to achieve the goal: If
the bearing angle is shrinking, increase speed or turn farther ahead of the
target; if it is growing, decrease speed or turn in the direction of the target.

Numerous studies have been conducted to test whether humans and other
animals use this constant bearing angle strategy. For readers who are interested
in this topic, the following papers offer useful entry points into this line of
research: Lenoir, Musch, Janssens, Thiery, and Uyttenhove (1999), Chardenon,
Montagne, Buekers, and Laurent (2002), Fajen and Warren (2004; 2007), Zhao,
Straub, and Rothkopf (2019). Readers who are interested in the use of the
constant bearing angle strategy in nonhuman animals should check out
Olberg, Worthington, and Venator (2000), and Ghose, Horiuchi,
Krishnaprasad, and Moss (2006).

4.2.2 Locomotor Interception of Aerial Targets (The Outfielder Problem)

An analogous solution exists for regulating running speed to catch a target
flying through the air. This task is most often framed in the context of running to
catch a fly ball and has come to be known as the outfielder problem. For our

purposes, it is sufficient to focus on the special case of a fly ball hit directly toward the outfielder so that the fielder needs to control forward or backward running speed but not move laterally. The fielder's current future refers to whether they will overshoot, undershoot, or arrive at the landing location in time to catch the ball if they continue to maintain their current speed. In 1968, physicist Seville Chapman (1968) demonstrated that this property is optically specified by the sign of the vertical acceleration of the ball's optical projection (or equivalently, the tangent of the ball's elevation angle φ; see Figure 11). If the ball is hit in front of the fielder and vertical acceleration is positive (i.e., $d^2 tan\varphi/dt^2 > 0$), the fielder is running too fast and will overshoot the landing location; if the vertical acceleration is negative (i.e., $d^2 tan\varphi/dt^2 < 0$), the fielder is running too slow and will undershoot. Thus, vertical acceleration specifies what will happen if the fielder maintains current running speed (i.e., the current future). By perceiving this property, the fielder can regulate running speed to cancel $d^2 tan\varphi/dt^2$ so as to arrive at the landing location at the same time as the ball. Readers who wish to learn more about research on the outfielder problem should check out Fink, Foo, and Warren (2009) as well as the earlier research cited in that paper.

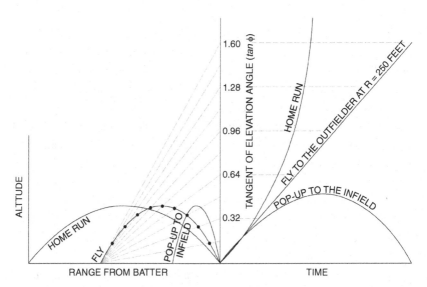

Figure 11 Diagram illustrating the OAC strategy. Reproduced from Chapman, S. (1968). Catching a baseball. *American Journal of Physics*, 36(10), 868–870, doi:10.1119/1.1974297, with the permission of the American Association of Physics Teachers.

4.2.3 Braking to Avoid a Collision

Another common task that involves online visual regulation of locomotion is decelerating to a stop to avoid collision with an object in the path of motion. Automobile drivers and cyclists perform this task on a routine basis, but it is common in nonhuman animals as well (e.g., flying insects and birds decelerate when landing on a surface to ensure soft contact). For this task, the current future refers to whether the actor will come to a stop before, at, or after reaching the target if they continue to maintain their current rate of deceleration. To perceive their current future, actors could rely on the optical variable τ, which readers will recall from Section 2.6 is equal to the ratio of the optical angle θ subtended by the approached object to its rate of change $\dot{\theta}$ (i.e., $\theta/\dot{\theta}$). Whereas τ specifies the time-to-contact with the approached object, the first derivative of τ (i.e., $\dot{\tau}$ or "tau-dot") specifies the sufficiency of the actor's current rate of deceleration for coming to a safe stop at the object; that is, the current future (Lee, 1976). Specifically, when the actor's current rate of deceleration is insufficient such that their speed will be greater than zero upon reaching the object, the value of $\dot{\tau}$ is less than –0.5. When current deceleration is excessive such that the actor will come to a stop before reaching the object, $\dot{\tau}$ is greater than –0.5. Thus, –0.5 is a critical value that separates conditions in which the actor is braking too little from conditions in which they are braking too hard. By detecting this information, actors can regulate deceleration to keep $\dot{\tau}$ as close as possible to –0.5, which ensures coming to a safe stop at the object (see Figure 12). Yilmaz and Warren (1995) tested the $\dot{\tau}$ hypothesis against three other hypotheses and found evidence to support the former.

Readers who are interested in the visual regulation of gait are encouraged to read about the current-future strategy for regulated stride length to step on a target, which was originally developed by David Lee (Lee et al., 1982) and further expanded and tested by others (see Barton, Matthis, & Fajen, 2017 for a review).

4.3 Affordance-Based Control

Not all information-based models assume that actors regulate locomotion by perceiving their current future. In this section, we will consider a contrasting view known as affordance-based control according to which locomotion is regulated by perceiving and realizing affordances (Fajen, 2005b; Fajen, 2007).

The main principle of affordance-based control is that actors select actions that are within their locomotor capabilities and regulate locomotion to ensure that the state (e.g., running speed, rate of deceleration) that is needed to successfully perform the task is always one that they are capable of attaining.

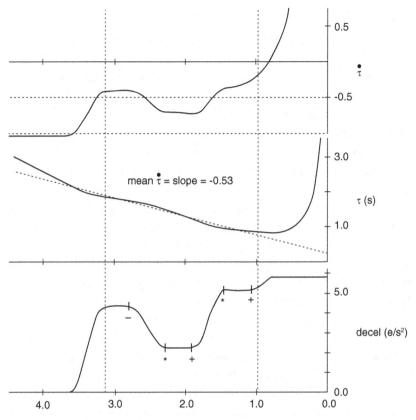

Figure 12 Diagram illustrating the tau-dot strategy. Subject increases rate of deceleration (bottom panel) whenever $\dot{\tau}$ is less than –0.5 (top panel) and vice versa. $\dot{\tau}$, τ, and rate of deceleration as a function of time leading up to the stop. From "Visual control of braking: A test of the $\dot{\tau}$ hypothesis," by E. H. Yilmaz and W. H. Warren, 1995, *Journal of Experimental Psychology: Human Perception and Performance*, 21(5), p. 1003. Copyright 1995 by the American Psychological Association. Reprinted with permission.

To make this idea more concrete, let us reconsider the task of running to catch a fly ball but now from the perspective of affordance-based control rather than current-future control. A fly ball is catchable if the fielder is capable of reaching the landing location before the ball hits the ground. In practice, this depends on a complex combination of variables such as the distance from the fielder to the landing location and the remaining flight time of the ball as well as the fielder's maximal running velocity and acceleration (Postma et al., 2018; Postma, 2019). For our purposes, it is sufficient to use an approximation of catchability based on two variables: the running speed needed to reach the landing location before the ball hits the ground (s_{req}) relative to the fielder's maximum running speed (S_{max}). Suppose that at the moment that the ball is hit, s_{req} is much less than S_{max}. At that moment, the ball is easily catchable. Before the fielder starts moving, s_{req} increases because the distance to the landing location remains the same as the remaining flight time decreases. Over time, if the fielder remains stationary, the ball becomes less and less catchable until, at some point, s_{req} exceeds S_{max} and the ball is uncatchable. Even if the fielder starts running toward the landing location, a ball that was once catchable could become uncatchable if they run too slowly. To keep the ball from becoming uncatchable, the fielder must run fast enough to maintain s_{req} below S_{max} – that is, they keep the speed needed to catch the ball below the maximum possible speed. As long as this condition is satisfied, it is always within the fielder's capabilities to catch the ball – that is, the affordance (catchability) can still be realized – and eventually, it will be realized. Thus, the control problem can be understood in terms of regulating running speed to ensure that the speed needed to catch the ball is always less than the maximum possible running speed (i.e., $s_{req} < S_{max}$).

Other visual guided locomotor tasks can also be reformulated in these terms. For example, the braking problem becomes one of regulating brake pressure to keep the deceleration needed to stop safely less than the maximum possible deceleration (Fajen, 2005c; Fajen, 2005a). Likewise, the interception problem becomes one of regulating locomotion to ensure that the speed needed to intercept the target is less than the maximum possible speed (Fajen, 2013; Bastin, Fajen, & Montagne, 2010).

4.3.1 Contrasting Affordance-Based and Current-Future Control

Although affordance-based control and current-future control share the assumption that visual guidance is information-based, they make different assumptions about the kinds of properties that actors must perceive to guide locomotion. Whereas affordance-based control assumes that actors perceive possibilities for action (e.g., whether a fly ball is catchable), current-future control assumes that actors perceive what will happen in the future if current conditions persist (e.g., whether the fielder will reach, overshoot, or undershoot the landing location if current running speed is maintained). Clearly, these are different properties. This is important because if visual guidance is in fact information-based, it is essential that we understand the nature of the information upon which actors rely to perform the task. The information that specifies affordances is very different from the information that specifies the current future. Thus, knowing whether locomotion is guided on the basis of affordances or the current future can help researchers decide what they should be looking for as they seek to identify the relevant information. To date, researchers have identified sources of information for the affordance-based control of braking (Fajen, 2005a) and locomotor interception (Fajen, 2013).

Affordance-based and current-future control also differ in terms of the degree to which behavior is constrained by the available visual information. Recall that current-future control asserts that actors regulate locomotion so as to bring about a particular pattern of optic flow, such as zero vertical optical acceleration in the case of running to catch a fly ball. In other words, there is a singular state of affairs that can be expressed in terms of available information (i.e., zero vertical optical acceleration) toward which behavior is adapted. This contrasts with affordance-based control, according to which locomotion is regulated to ensure that the state (e.g., running speed, rate of deceleration) that is needed to successfully perform the task is always one that is possible to achieve. In other words, rather than a specific desired state, there is a range of states (i.e., a safe zone) within which the actor attempts to remain.

Whether a control strategy should prescribe a specific state or a range of states is a matter of debate. A proponent of the current-future account might argue that current-future models make specific testable predictions about how actors should regulate locomotion at each moment and explain why one specific movement trajectory emerges. A supporter of affordance-based control might argue that current-future models are too rigid and leave no room for the kind of flexibility that actors often need to accommodate the demands of a specific situation. In baseball, for example, outfielders sometimes need to arrive at the landing location in advance and wait for the ball to arrive; other times they approach gradually at first and then sprint forward at the last moment to catch the ball on the run, which allows them to make a stronger throw back to the infield. Similarly, when a driver approaches a stop sign, they may prioritize their passengers' safety and comfort by initiating braking early on and decelerating gradually or they may be in a hurry and wait until the last moment before slamming on the brakes. The ability to vary the manner in which a task is performed is central to adaptive behavior, but such flexibility often entails regulating locomotion in ways that differ from what current-future models predict.

A third point of departure for affordance-based and current-future models concerns the treatment of action selection and online visual guidance. In this context, action selection refers to the choices that actors make about whether to initiate an action and, once it is initiated, whether to continue to execute that action. For example, in the wild, predators must be selective about which prey animals to pursue. If the prey is too far away or moving quickly toward a place where it can escape (e.g., a burrow), chasing the animal is a waste of valuable energy resources. Such decisions fall outside the scope of current-future models, which are intended to account for online visual guidance but not action selection. In other words, current-future models treat action selection and visual guidance as separate processes (see Warren, 1988). In contrast, affordance-based models have the potential to explain both aspects of the task. That is, the same information that is used to guide locomotion while chasing a moving target could also be used to decide whether to initiate pursuit and whether to continue to pursue the target (Steinmetz, Layton, Powell, & Fajen, 2020).

4.4 Behavioral Dynamics

Recall that one of the core assertions of information-based control is that behavior is not planned in advance but rather emerges from the coupling of informational variables to action variables. This idea was further advanced through a synthesis of information-based control with the dynamical systems approach to the study of coordination dynamics (Jirsa & Kelso, 2004; Kelso, 1995; Turvey, 1990). The result is a rich theoretical framework known as behavioral dynamics (Warren, 2006) within which various forms of locomotor behavior can be understood and modeled. Behavioral dynamics explicitly rejects the notion that locomotion is centrally controlled as well as the assumption that the organization of behavior can be attributed to some internal structure (e.g., a brain region, a neural circuit, a motor program). Rather, behavior is self-organized.

The general framework is depicted in Figure 13. Both the agent and the environment are treated as dynamical systems – that is, as systems whose states evolve over time – whose behavior can be captured by a system of differential equations (see Strogatz, 2001 for an excellent introduction). Although it is common to characterize the environment in these terms, the agent can also be described as a dynamical system. During a given task, such as walking, the many neuromuscular and biomechanical degrees of freedom of the agent's action system become coordinated through the formation of synergies (Latash, 2008; Turvey, 1990; Turvey, 2007; Turvey & Carello, 1996). As such, it behaves as a low-dimensional dynamical system. In other words, the intrinsic dynamics of the action system can be captured in terms of a small number of states that evolve over time.

As shown by the arrows pointing between agent and environment in Figure 13, the agent's states are influenced by the environment through perceptual information and the agent influences the states of the environment through action. What emerges from these interactions is behavior, which can be captured in terms of trajectories through a state space of behavioral variables (top right of

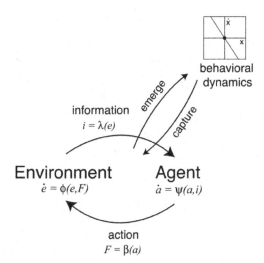

Figure 13 Depiction of behavioral dynamics emerging from and capturing interactions between agent and environment. From "The dynamics of perception and action," by W. H. Warren, 2006, *Psychological Review*, 113(2), p. 367. Copyright 2006 by the American Psychological Association. Reprinted with permission.

Figure 13). These behavioral trajectories are determined by the layout of attractors, which correspond to desired states, and repellors, which correspond to avoided states. Changes in the number or stability of attractors and repellors can also occur. These correspond to transitions in behavior and are called bifurcations.

We can now better appreciate what visual control means within this framework. The primary means by which the agent influences behavior is through changes in the mappings from informational variables to action system variables. These mappings, which are represented by the function ψ in Figure 13, correspond to laws of control (see Section 4.1). By learning new mappings and adjusting the parameters of existing mappings, the agent can bring about changes at the level of behavioral dynamics so that the behavior that emerges is what the agent desires (Warren, 2006). That is, by properly tuning the control law, the agent can alter the behavioral landscape such that trajectories converge toward desired states (e.g., goals) and diverge away from avoided states (e.g., obstacles). Thus, behavior is not dictated by a central controller, but neither is the agent a slave to the dynamics, incapable of exerting any influence on the emergent behavior. Rather, "the agent modulates the dynamics of the system in which it is embedded via the lever at its disposal – a control law – to enact a stable and adaptive task solution" (Warren, 2006, p. 385).

4.4.1 The Behavioral Dynamics of Steering, Obstacle Avoidance, and Route Selection

This is all very abstract but can be made more intuitive with a concrete example: the task of walking to a stationary goal while avoiding a stationary obstacle (Fajen & Warren, 2003). The desired states for this task are those in which the agent is moving on a straight path toward the goal and the states to be avoided are those in which the agent is heading toward an obstacle. The directions of the goal and obstacle behave as attractors and repellors respectively of the agent's heading. It is as if the agent's heading is being pulled into alignment with the goal by a damped spring and simultaneously pushed out of alignment with the obstacle by a second spring (see Figure 14).

Experiments with human subjects walking toward goals and avoiding obstacles revealed how the attraction of goals and the repulsion of obstacles vary as a function of the distance to these objects and their angle relative to heading (Fajen & Warren, 2003). For example, goals attract the agent's heading more strongly when they are nearby and at larger angles. Likewise, obstacles repel the agent's heading more strongly when they are nearby and at smaller angles.

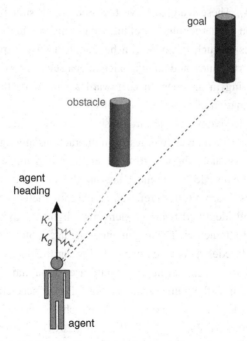

Figure 14 Behavioral dynamics of steering and obstacle avoidance. Adapted from Figure 2 of Warren (2018). Color version of figure available at www .cambridge.org/fajen

Things start to get interesting when goals and obstacles are in competition. For example, in the scenario depicted in Figure 14, the goal draws the agent's heading in the clockwise direction while the obstacle pushes it counterclockwise. Which of these objects exerts a stronger influence on the agent determines the change in heading at each instant and ultimately, the route that the agent takes to the goal – that is, whether it follows an outside path to the left of the obstacle or an inside path to the right. However, because the strength of goal attraction and obstacle repulsion varies with the angle and distance to these objects, the relative influence of these objects varies as the agent moves. Thus, the route is not chosen at the outset but rather emerges in real time as the agent moves. Furthermore, the model scales up to predict human route selection in more complex scenarios involving multiple obstacles (Warren & Fajen, 2004; Warren & Fajen, 2008).

4.4.2 The Behavioral Dynamics of Crowds

The behavioral dynamics approach has also been extended to capture behavior involving moving objects, such as interception (Fajen & Warren, 2007) and pedestrian following (Dachner & Warren, 2014; Rio, Rhea, & Warren, 2014; Rio et al., 2014). These features leave the model well suited to capture the collective motion of a larger number of individuals moving in a crowd (Warren, 2018). Examples of such behavior can be found in busy airports, shopping malls, and concert venues, and include phenomena such as common motion of pedestrians moving in an open space toward a similar destination and the spontaneous formation of opposing lanes of flow.

Studies of collective motion in birds, fish, and humans suggest that coherent motion at the global level emerges from interactions among individuals at the local level. As such, the key to understanding and modeling collective motion at the global scale lies in understanding the local interactions between individual agents. Warren (2018) referred to these interactions as the "rules of engagement" and identified two key elements: alignment dynamics and the neighborhood of interaction. The alignment dynamics capture the interactions between pairs of pedestrians when one is following the other. Of the several possible control strategies that humans could use to maintain alignment, the one that best captures the human data has the follower accelerate or decelerate to match the leader's speed and turn to match the leader's heading (see Figure 15) (Dachner & Warren, 2014; Rio et al., 2014). The neighborhood of influence broadens the scope to capture how each individual is influenced by the multiple neighbors that surround them. The effects of each neighbor within an individual's field of view combine linearly, but not all neighbors

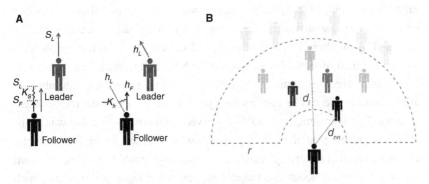

Figure 15 Alignment dynamics (left) and neighborhood of influence. Reprinted from Figure 2 and Figure 6 from Warren (2018).

exert an equal influence. The greater the distance between the individual and their neighbor, the weaker is the coupling. Interestingly, the drop-off in coupling strength with distance is slightly more complicated than a simple exponential decay model could capture because the influence of any given neighbor also depends on how far away the other neighbors are. For example, in a crowd with four neighbors, a neighbor at 5 m exerts a greater influence if the other three neighbors lie beyond 5 m than if they all lie within 5 m. Rather than a simple exponential decay, Warren proposed that the drop-off in coupling strength with distance is best captured by a donut model with two decay rates – a slow decay to the nearest neighbor in the crowd and a faster decay within the crowd.

Taken together, alignment dynamics and neighborhood of interaction are sufficient to simulate globally coherent motion among multiple agents. In computer simulations with 30 agents with random initial headings and speeds, the agents eventually organized themselves into a crowd moving at a common speed and direction (Warren, 2018). Although there are many other models of collective motion, the approach described here is somewhat distinct in that the local interactions are grounded in actual human behavior observed in controlled experiments. Thus, by understanding the rules of engagement that govern local interactions, the coherent motion exhibited by human crowds can be understood as an emergent, self-organized phenomenon.

5 The Internal-Model Debate

Up to this point, our analysis of visual control has been from the information-based perspective. Information-based control is an account of how actions are controlled under conditions in which information is currently available (so-called "online control"). It does not purport to explain the control of action when information is unavailable, such as when a moving target becomes briefly occluded by another object or when a shift in gaze moves a nearby obstacle outside the field of view. To account for such behavior, one might posit some kind of internal representation or internal model that persists even in the absence of information and can be continually updated as the state of the environment changes. This representation could be derived from information that was available in the recent past along with prior knowledge of the world. For example, a representation of a recently occluded moving target could be constructed from visual information about the target's motion prior to occlusion along with knowledge of how such targets tend to move.

The notion that action is controlled on the basis of an internal model is known as model-based control (Loomis & Beall, 2004). Over the past few decades, the hypothesis that humans and other animals construct and use internal models during the control of locomotion has been the focal point of an ongoing debate (see Zhao & Warren, 2015 for a recent review). The aim of this section is to introduce readers to this debate. First, we will consider what exactly is meant by an internal model and the putative roles that such models may play in the control of locomotion. Second, we will explore the issues and questions that have been at the center of the debate. Lastly, we will consider the empirical evidence and theoretical arguments that favor one side or the other.

5.1 What Is (and Is Not) an Internal Model?

One of the critical steps in eventually resolving the internal-model debate is establishing a clear definition of the term so that researchers can agree on what does and does not constitute an internal model. In this section, we identify two key properties.

The first, which originated with Craik (1943), is the notion that internal models simulate events in the external world. They internalize the laws of physics and can be likened to the physics engines used by computer programmers to simulate events in virtual environments, such as collisions, the movement of systems with interconnected components acting under external forces (i.e., rigid-body dynamics), and the movement of deformable objects and fluids (Battaglia, Hamrick, & Tenenbaum, 2013). Craik proposed that by predicting the consequences of various possible actions, organisms could test out different alternatives and choose the one that was best. Internal models could also serve to prepare organisms for events that are likely to happen in the future (see McNamee & Wolpert, 2019 for a recent discussion of the various roles that internal models could play in the control of movement).

The second key characteristic of internal models is that they can "stand in" for some external state of affairs. Although they may be constructed and updated by perceptual information, they are not wholly dependent on information for their continued existence. Even if information about the environment is unavailable for some period of time, internal models can continue to play a causal role in the guidance of locomotion.

With these two characteristics in mind, let us consider a paradigmatic example of an internal model: a mechanism that predicts the future trajectory of a moving object such as a ball flying through the air or rolling across the field. Such a model could take as input visual information about the current state of the object and generate predictions using such information along with internalized knowledge of how objects move in a gravitational field and how they are affected by air resistance, wind, and friction. Even if visual information becomes unavailable, an internal model would continue to predict the motion of the ball.

It is also instructive to consider things that might, at first glance, seem to meet the criteria for internal models but do not. An information-based control law of the sort described in Section 4 is not an internal model because it does not possess either of the two key properties. Control laws do not simulate the external world and they do not serve to guide behavior when information is unavailable (Warren, 2006). Constants to which one could become perceptually attuned, such as gravity or limits on action capabilities (e.g., maximum running speed), do correspond to external states and persist in the absence of information but do not by themselves simulate events.

5.2 The Internal-Model Debate

Now that we have clarified what an internal model is and is not, let us return to the internal-model debate and examine the source of the controversy. Information-based control and model-based control have distinct natural domains that they purportedly explain best (Zhao & Warren, 2015). The natural domain for information-based control is tasks in which locomotion can be guided by currently available information (i.e., online control). For model-based control, the natural domain is tasks in which locomotion must be controlled in the absence of information (i.e., off-line control). Given these differences, it might not be obvious why there is any controversy at all. Prima facie, there seems to be no reason why these two types of control could not be considered complementary and understood as explanations of different phenomena (i.e., actors rely on information when it is available and switch to an internal model when information is absent). Although this would avoid controversy, such an account is unsatisfying to proponents of both theories and leaves both sides craving something more parsimonious.

One alternative is to reject information-based control and expand the scope of model-based control by asserting that internal models play a critical role even when information is available. The appeal is a single, unified theory that explains both online and off-line control. According to this account, perceptual information is used to construct and update an internal model of the environment, which in turn is used to plan actions. In other words, internal models are a link in the causal chain between perception and action (Loomis & Beall, 1998; Loomis & Beall, 2004). Hence, the success with which we move about is largely rooted in the close correspondence between internal models and the real world. To validate this account, one would need to demonstrate that internal models are sufficiently accurate and robust to account for behavior. One would also need to show that there are certain aspects of behavior during online control tasks, such as the ability to guide locomotion in anticipation of future events, for which information alone is not sufficient and internal models are needed.

Alternatively, one could reject model-based control and assert that internal models are not necessary to account for behavior even in the absence of information. This approach is sometimes motivated by philosophical arguments against internal representations in general. The hypothesis has also been criticized for being too ill-defined to empirically test. For example, it assumes a mechanism capable of generating model-based predictions but does not specify the accuracy of such predictions. Likewise, it assumes a mechanism that persists without degradation in the absence of information but does not specify the duration of persistence. To support the nonrepresentationalist position, one would need to show that information-based control is sufficient to account for the guidance of locomotion when information is available as well as develop a plausible account of behavior during off-line control that does not involve internal models.

5.3 Empirical Evidence and Theoretical Arguments

Can model-based control provide a seamless account of both online and off-line control, or should researchers seek to eliminate internal models altogether from their accounts of visual control? In this section, we will examine the empirical evidence and theoretical arguments. The goal is not to settle the debate but rather to examine the case for both sides.

5.3.1 Off-Line Control: Are Internal Models Necessary and Sufficient to Explain Behavior in the Absence of Information?

Model-based control attributes the general success with which we move about in complex environments to the existence of internal models that closely correspond to the environment and persist for some period of time in the absence of information. As such, one avenue for corroborating the model-based approach is to look for evidence of internal models that are both accurate and durable. The most relevant evidence comes from studies of visually directed actions, in which visual information is initially available but then cut off before the action is initiated. A widely used task, known as blind walking, requires subjects to briefly view a target on the ground, close their eyes, and walk to the target's location (Loomis, Da Silva, Fujita, & Fukusima, 1992; Rieser, Ashmead, Talor, & Youngquist, 1990; Thomson, 1983). The results of these studies demonstrate that humans are capable of blindly walking to targets up to 24 m away with no systematic biases and small variable error (~8 percent of target distance in Rieser et al., 1990). Follow-up studies demonstrate considerable flexibility in the ability to guide locomotion without concurrent visual information. For example, subjects are capable of blindly walking to a previously viewed target even after walking in a different direction for an unpredictable distance until cued by the experimenter to turn and walk toward the target (Fukusima, Loomis, & Da Silva, 1997; Philbeck, Loomis, & Beall, 1997). For proponents of model-based control, such findings taken together provide evidence of internal models that accurately represent the spatial layout of the world, resist rapid degradation in the absence of visual information, and are continually updated based on changes in position that are sensed by non-visual information.

These conclusions, however, are challenged by the results of other studies using tasks with greater spatial-temporal demands. For example, when subjects attempted to intercept a moving target that sometimes moved behind an opaque wall, they stopped making adaptive steering adjustments once the target was occluded and instead continued to walk in approximately the same direction (Zhao & Warren, 2017). Such findings are difficult to reconcile with model-based accounts, which assume mechanisms that predict target trajectory even during brief periods of occlusion.

Studies of open-loop driving, in which subjects perform routine driving maneuvers such as negotiating a curve (Macuga, Beall, Smith, & Loomis, 2019; Godthelp, 1986), changing lanes (Godthelp, 1985; Wallis, Chatziastros, & Bülthoff, 2002b), or correcting position within a lane (Hildreth, Beusmans, Boer, & Royden, 2000) while visual information is temporarily occluded, also bear on questions about the necessity and sufficiency of internal models. Interestingly, although most of these studies were conducted in a driving simulator, there are a few real-world exceptions, the most notable of which is a 1967, Ig-Nobel-prize-winning study by human factors pioneer John Senders (Senders, Kristofferson, Levison, Dietrich, & Ward, 1967). Senders assembled a helmet with an opaque visor that flapped down and up to intermittently blind the driver. An engrossing video of Senders himself demonstrating the apparatus while driving on a highway outside of Boston can be found on the internet.

In many studies of open-loop driving, subjects were able to perform the required maneuver with minimal error for short occlusion durations, but performance started to deteriorate when vision was occluded for more than 1–2 s. Such findings weaken the case for model-based control because, if internal models are so dependent on continuously available information, it is unclear why they would be constructed in the first place (Zhao & Warren, 2015). Perhaps the most compelling result from this body of research comes from a study by Wallis et al. (2002a) in which subjects in a driving simulator were instructed to change lanes after driving into a completely dark tunnel. Changing lanes is a well-practiced maneuver for experienced drivers, and the task in Wallis et al. required subjects to perform a lane change in full daylight moments prior to entering the tunnel. Nevertheless, subjects consistently failed to complete the entire sequence of steering wheel rotations needed to successfully change lanes. Importantly, it was not that subjects failed to turn the wheel far enough. Rather, changing lanes involves three distinct segments of steering wheel changes, and subjects completed only 1½ of them (compare diagrams in lower left and lower right of Figure 16). When they had brought the steering wheel back to center and thought they had completed the lane change, they were actually heading at an oblique angle across the highway and off the edge of the road. The diagram at the top of Figure 16 illustrates the trajectories that subjects would have taken if they were not in the tunnel when they changed lanes. Such findings pose a challenge to model-based accounts, which rely on accurate internal models of not only the spatial layout but also the dynamics and dimensions of the vehicle, body, and so on (Loomis & Beall, 2004). Rather than internalizing the dynamics of the steering wheel, drivers apparently adopt a strategy that relies on information, which is continuously available under most circumstances outside the laboratory.

The research just described aims to examine the sufficiency of internal models to account for behavior in the absence of visual information. Let us now turn the question of whether internal models are necessary. Might it be possible to explain how actors control locomotion during periods of occlusion without resorting to internal models? We will revisit the outfielder problem but this time imagine that the ball's trajectory is affected by a crosswind blowing from left to right (Zhao & Warren, 2015). In general, experienced fielders have little difficulty adapting their running trajectory to the flight of the ball under such conditions, even if they must occasionally shift their gaze away from the ball (e.g., to avoid colliding with the wall). For the present purposes, the

Figure 16 The top diagram is a screenshot of the simulated driving environment with trajectories superimposed over a roadway. Bottom diagrams show steering wheel maneuvers required for lane change (left) and exhibited by subjects (right). Reprinted from *Current Biology*, 12(4), Wallis, G., Chatziastros, A., & Bülthoff, H., "An unexpected role for visual feedback in vehicle steering control", 295–299, Copyright 2002, with permission from Elsevier. Color version of figure available at www.cambridge.org/fajen

relevant question is how the fielder guides locomotion during these periods of decoupling. Proponents of model-based control contend that the fielder relies on a prediction of the ball's trajectory that takes into account the relevant forces that act upon it as it moves, which in this example includes not only gravity but also the crosswind. However, the ability to guide locomotion during periods of occlusion may also be captured by simpler strategies (Zhao & Warren, 2015). For example, the fielder could learn from previous experience that when the ball goes out of view, they should veer slightly in the direction that the wind is blowing. Zhao and Warren (2015) referred to this strategy as a heuristic and argued that it does not meet the criteria for an internal model because it does not involve internally simulating states of the world, such as the ball's trajectory.

Whether the control of locomotion under such conditions is better captured by an internal model or a simpler strategy remains an interesting open question. Both hypotheses need to be further fleshed out so that predictions can be derived and empirically tested.

5.3.2 Online Control: Do Internal Models Play a Role When Information Is Available?

One approach to determining whether internal models are needed during online control uses modeling and simulation of information-based control strategies to assess the sufficiency of currently available information (Zhao & Warren, 2015). If such models can capture human behavior, then at least in principle, information alone is sufficient and internal models are not needed. On the other hand, if there are aspects of human behavior that cannot be captured by such models, then information alone is insufficient. An example of this approach is the model of behavioral dynamics of steering, obstacle avoidance, and route selection described in Section 4.4.1 (Fajen & Warren, 2003; Fajen & Warren, 2007; Warren & Fajen, 2008). Simulations of this model provide an existence proof that internal models are not necessary to explain certain key locomotor behaviors, including the ability to choose routes around obstacles in a humanlike manner.

Modeling and simulation is a useful approach, but it does not prove the case against a role for internal models during online control. The idea that locomotion is directly coupled to currently available information in optic flow has been challenged by demonstrating that the control of self-motion can be affected by manipulations of perceived self-motion that leave optic flow unaffected (Kelly, Loomis, & Beall, 2005; Mohler et al., 2007). In addition, there are other aspects of online locomotor control, such as certain behaviors involved in locomotor interception (discussed below), that are not currently well captured by information-based models. Whether information-based models can be adapted to better capture these aspects of behavior remains an open question.

We have already learned about locomotor interception from an information-based perspective – by moving so as to maintain a constant bearing angle, the actor will eventually intercept the target (see Section 4.2.1). According to this account, currently available information is sufficient to guide locomotion in anticipation of the future. Proponents of model-based control challenge this claim and contend that locomotor interception also relies on prediction of the future states, such as where the target will be in the future and how self-motion will affect the optical motion of the target.

The two accounts predict similar behavior in many scenarios but can be teased apart by studying behavior in situations in which targets change speeds or directions. Consider, for example, the task shown in Figure 17, in which the subject is instructed to intercept a target moving along a straight trajectory or one of several curvilinear trajectories all of which intersect the subject's walking path at the same location (Bastin, Craig, & Montagne, 2006). If subjects relied on a model-based prediction and were able to accurately predict the future trajectory of the target up to the intersection point, walking behavior should be the same for each of the five conditions shown in Figure 17 because the target arrives at the same intersection point at the same time. On the other hand, if walking speed is controlled based on currently available information by nulling the change in bearing angle, subjects should walk at different speeds depending on whether the target's path curvature is positive or negative. The results fall in between the predictions of these two hypotheses (Diaz, Phillips, & Fajen, 2009). Whether this reflects the use of an internal model or a simpler heuristic remains an interesting open question (Bootsma, Ledouit, Casanova, & Zaal, 2016; Zhao & Warren, 2015; Morice, François, Jacobs, & Montagne, 2010).

The possible role of internal models during interception has also been investigated in nonhuman animals, including invertebrates. In an elegant study, Mischiati et al. (2015) used motion capture to record how dragonflies moved their body and head and what they saw as they flew through an arena to capture their prey. They found that steering movements were not consistent with reactive (i.e., information-based) control models driven by prey image motion alone. As dragonflies fly toward their prey, they orient their bodies to maximize speed and maneuverability and to minimize the need for rapid turns during the

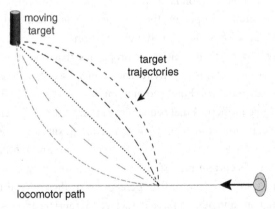

Figure 17 Moving observer walking to intercept a target moving along one of five possible trajectories (some of which are curved). Adapted from *Human Movement Science*, 25(6), Bastin, J., Craig, C., & Montagne, G., "Prospective strategies underlie the control of interceptive actions," 718–732. Copyright 2006, with permission from Elsevier.

moments immediately preceding capture. Such body orientation changes as well as changes in the relative motion between the dragonfly and prey would cause the image of the prey to drift on the dragonfly's eyes. However, dragonflies rotate their heads to counteract the optical effects of such movements, keeping the prey image at a fixed location on the eyes, which the authors referred to as "prey foveation." Importantly, such movements occur with nearly zero lag. This is difficult to reconcile with accounts based on reactions to sensory feedback (e.g., drift of the prey image on the dragonfly's eyes), which one would expect to lag behind due to inherent delays in the sensorimotor and neuromuscular systems. Instead, the authors concluded that dragonflies rely on an internal forward model to predict prey image drift using an efference copy of the motor commands to the wings, and an internal inverse model to compute the motor commands to the head that are needed to cancel out the predicted disturbance. An open question about the internal model account is how dragonflies know the absolute distance to the target, which is needed to predict prey image drift. Olberg, Worthington, Fox, Bessette, and Loosemore (Olberg, Worthington, Fox, Bessette, & Loosemore, 2005) reported evidence that perching dragonflies are able to estimate distance, but it is unknown how they do so and whether they can estimate distance while in flight.

6 Concluding Remarks

Beyond presenting an integrative summary of research on the perception and control of self-motion, this Element was written to raise awareness that the primary function of perception is to enable animals to move around in cluttered environments. From this perspective, the most important properties to be perceived are those that are immediately relevant to the control of action. These are not limited to the kinds of properties that one normally uses to describe the current state of the environment, such as distances, sizes, surface orientations, and velocities. For a moving animal, survival may depend on the ability to perceive properties that reflect the moving observer's relation to their environment (e.g., time-to-contact with an upcoming surface), possibilities for action (e.g., the cross-ability of a busy street), or current future (e.g., the sufficiency of one's current rate of deceleration for avoiding collision with an obstacle in the path of motion). The perception of these properties makes it possible for humans and other animals to select appropriate actions and regulate locomotion in a way that takes into account the dynamics and dimensions of the body and the environment.

Looking ahead, advances in the study of visually guided locomotion will occur when researchers glean new insights into the properties that must be perceived to regulate locomotion, the sources of information that specify those properties, the mechanisms that allow for the detection of such information, and the strategies that map information onto control. Some advances will undoubtedly be driven by developments in technology that make it possible to study visual control in more naturalistic environments and in the context of more complex, real-world tasks, just as they have in the recent past with improvements in computer graphics, virtual reality, motion capture, and mobile eye tracking. The opportunity to study visual control in more naturalistic settings will allow us to integrate fragmented knowledge of how individual components of a task are executed into more unified models that capture the entire set of behaviors that are involved in real-world tasks (Lappi & Mole, 2018; Hayhoe, 2017). Advances may also be driven by exploring one of the many possible applications of research on visually guided locomotion, such as semiautonomous vehicles (Mole et al., 2019), mobile robotics (Escobar-Alvarez et al., 2017; Floreano, Zufferey, Klaptocz, Germann, & Kovac, 2017; Floreano, Ijspeert, & Schaal, 2014; Srinivasan, 2011), and improving mobility in individuals with visual and motor impairments (Kuo & Donelan, 2010).

References

Adolph, K. E. (2008a). The growing body in action: What infant locomotion tells us about perceptually guided action. In R. Klatzky, B. MacWhinney, & M. Behrmann (eds.), *Embodiment, Ego-Space, and Action* (pp. 275–321). Psychology Press.

Adolph, K. E. (2008b). Learning to move. *Current Directions in Psychological Science*, 17(3), 213–218. doi:10.1111/j.1467-8721.2008.00577.x

Angelaki, D. E., Gu, Y., & Deangelis, G. C. (2011). Visual and vestibular cue integration for heading perception in extrastriate visual cortex. *J. Physiol.*, 589(Pt 4), 825–833. doi:10.1113/jphysiol.2010.194720

Banks, M. S., Ehrlich, S. M., Backus, B. T., & Crowell, J. A. (1996). Estimating heading during real and simulated eye movements. *Vision Research*, 36(3), 431–443. doi:10.1016/0042-6989(95)00122-0

Barsingerhorn, A. D., Zaal, F. T. J. M., Smith, J., & Pepping, G.-J. (2012). On possibilities for action: the past, present and future of affordance research. *Avant*, 3(2).

Barton, S. L., Matthis, J. S., & Fajen, B. R. (2017). Visual regulation of gait: zeroing in on a solution to the complex terrain problem. *Journal of Experimental Psychology: Human Perception and Performance*, 43(10), 1773–1790. doi:10.1037/xhp0000435

Bastin, J., Craig, C., & Montagne, G. (2006). Prospective strategies underlie the control of interceptive actions. *Hum. Mov. Sci.*, 25(6), 718–732. doi:10.1016/j.humov.2006.04.001

Bastin, J., Fajen, B. R., & Montagne, G. (2010). Controlling speed and direction during interception: an affordance-based approach. *Exp. Brain Res.*, 201(4), 763–780. doi:10.1007/s00221-009-2092-y

Battaglia, P. W., Hamrick, J. B., & Tenenbaum, J. B. (2013). Simulation as an engine of physical scene understanding. *Proc. Natl. Acad. Sci. U S A*, 110 (45), 18327–18332. doi:10.1073/pnas.1306572110

Bootsma, R. J. (2009). The (current) future is here! *Perception*, 38(6), 851.

Bootsma, R. J., Ledouit, S., Casanova, R., & Zaal, F. T. J. M. (2016). Fractional-order information in the visual control of lateral locomotor interception. *Journal of Experimental Psychology: Human Perception and Performance*, 42(4), 517–529. doi:10.1037/xhp0000162

Britten, K. H. (2008). Mechanisms of self-motion perception. *Annu. Rev. Neurosci.*, 31, 389–410. doi:10.1146/annurev.neuro.29.051605.112953

Britten, K. H., & van Wezel, R. J. A. (1998). Electrical microstimulation of cortical area MST biases heading perception in monkeys. *Nature Neuroscience*, 1, 59–63.

Chapman, S. (1968). Catching a baseball. *American Journal of Physics*, 36(10), 868–870. doi:10.1119/1.1974297

Chardenon, A., Montagne, G., Buekers, M. J., & Laurent, M. (2002). The visual control of ball interception during human locomotion. *Neuroscience Letters*, 334(1), 13–16.

Cheng, J. C. K., & Li, L. (2012). Effects of reference objects and extra-retinal information about pursuit eye movements on curvilinear path perception from retinal flow. *Journal of Vision*, 12(3):12, 1–21. doi:10.1167/12.3.12

Craik, K. J. W. (1943). *The Nature of Explanation*. Cambridge, UK: Cambridge University Press.

Creem-Regehr, S. H., Stefanucci, J. K., & Thompson, W. B. (2015). Perceiving absolute scale in virtual environments: How theory and application have mutually informed the role of body-based perception. In *Psychology of Learning and Motivation*, 62 (pp. 195–224). Elsevier.

Cullen, K. E. (2019). Vestibular processing during natural self-motion: implications for perception and action. *Nature Reviews Neuroscience*, 20(6), 346–363. doi:10.1038/s41583-019-0153-1

Cuturi, L. F., & MacNeilage, P. R. (2013). Systematic biases in human heading estimation. *PLoS ONE*, 8(2), e56862.

Dachner, G. C., & Warren, W. H. (2014). Behavioral dynamics of heading alignment in pedestrian following. *Transportation Research Procedia*, 2, 69–76. doi:10.1016/j.trpro.2014.09.010

Diaz, G. J., Phillips, F., & Fajen, B. R. (2009). Intercepting moving targets: a little foresight helps a lot. *Experimental Brain Research*, 195(3), 345–360. doi:10.1007/s00221-009-1794-5

Dixon, M. W., Wraga, M., Proffitt, D. R., & Williams, G. C. (2000). Eye height scaling of absolute size in immersive and nonimmersive displays. *Journal of Experimental Psychology: Human Perception and Performance*, 26(2), 582.

Dokka, K., DeAngelis, G. C., & Angelaki, D. E. (2015). Multisensory integration of visual and vestibular signals improves heading discrimination in the presence of a moving object. *Journal of Neuroscience*, 35(40), 13599–13607. doi:10.1523/JNEUROSCI.2267-15.2015

Dokka, K., MacNeilage, P. R., DeAngelis, G. C., & Angelaki, D. E. (2013). Multisensory self-motion compensation during object trajectory judgments. *Cerebral Cortex*.

Dokka, K., Park, H., Jansen, M., DeAngelis, G. C., & Angelaki, D. E. (2019). Causal inference accounts for heading perception in the presence of object motion. *Proc. Natl. Acad. Sci. U S A*, 116(18), 9060–9065. doi:10.1073/pnas.1820373116

Duffy, C. J., & Wurtz, R. H. (1991). Sensitivity of MST neurons to optic flow stimuli. I. A continuum of response selectivity to large-field stimuli. *Journal of Neurophysiology*, 65(6), 1329–1345.

Durant, S., & Zanker, J. M. (2020). The combined effect of eye movements improve head centred local motion information during walking. *PLoS One*, 15(1), e0228345. doi:10.1371/journal.pone.0228345

Elder, D. M., Grossberg, S., & Mingolla, E. (2009). A neural model of visually guided steering, obstacle avoidance, and route selection. *Journal of Experimental Psychology: Human Perception and Performance*, 35(5), 1501–1531.

Escobar-Alvarez, H. D., Johnson, N., Hebble, T., Klingebiel, K., Quintero, S. A. P., Regenstein, J., & Browning, N. A. (2017). R-ADVANCE: Rapid adaptive prediction for vision-based autonomous navigation, control, and evasion. *Journal of Field Robotics*, 35(1), 91–100. doi:10.1002/rob.21744

Fajen, B. R. (2005a). Calibration, information, and control strategies for braking to avoid a collision. *Journal of Experimental Psychology: Human Perception and Performance*, 31(3), 480–501. doi:10.1037/0096-1523.31.3.480

Fajen, B. R. (2005b). Perceiving possibilities for action: On the necessity of calibration and perceptual learning for the visual guidance of action. *Perception*, 34, 717–740. doi:10.1068/p5405

Fajen, B. R. (2005c). The scaling of information to action in visually guided braking. *Journal of Experimental Psychology: Human Perception and Performance*, 31(5), 1107–1123. doi:10.1037/0096-1523.31.5.1107

Fajen, B. R. (2007). Affordance-based control of visually guided action. *Ecological Psychology*, 19(4), 383–410.

Fajen, B. R. (2013). Guiding locomotion in complex, dynamic environments. *Frontiers in Behavioral Neuroscience*, 7(Article 85), 1–15. doi:10.3389/fnbeh.2013.00085/abstract

Fajen, B. R., Diaz, G., & Cramer, C. (2011). Reconsidering the role of movement in perceiving action-scaled affordances. *Human Movement Science*, 30(3), 504–533. doi:10.1016/j.humov.2010.07.016

Fajen, B. R., & Matthis, J. S. (2011). Direct perception of action-scaled affordances: The shrinking gap problem. *Journal of Experimental Psychology: Human Perception and Performance*, 37(5), 1442.

Fajen, B. R., & Matthis, J. S. (2013). Visual and non-visual contributions to the perception of object motion during self-motion. *PLoS One*, 8(2), e55446. doi:10.1371/journal.pone.0055446

Fajen, B. R., Parade, M. S., & Matthis, J. S. (2013). Humans perceive object motion in world coordinates during obstacle avoidance. *J Vis*, 13(8). doi:10.1167/13.8.25

Fajen, B. R., Riley, M. A., & Turvey, M. T. (2008). Information, affordances, and the control of action in sport. *International Journal of Sport Psychology*, 40, 79–107.

Fajen, B. R., & Turvey, M. T. (2003). Perception, categories, and possibilities for action. *Adaptive Behavior*, 11(4), 276–278.

Fajen, B. R., & Warren, W. H. (2003). Behavioral dynamics of steering, obstable avoidance, and route selection. *Journal of Experimental Psychology: Human Perception and Performance*, 29(2), 343–362.

Fajen, B. R., & Warren, W. H. (2004). Visual guidance of intercepting a moving target on foot. *Perception*, 33(6), 689–715. doi:10.1068/p5236

Fajen, B. R., & Warren, W. H. (2007). Behavioral dynamics of intercepting a moving target. *Experimental Brain Research*, 180(2), 303–319. doi:10.1007/s00221-007-0859-6

Fath, A. J., & Fajen, B. R. (2011). Static and dynamic visual information about the size and passability of an aperture. *Perception*, 40(8), 887–904. doi:10.1068/p6917

Fink, P. W., Foo, P. S., & Warren, W. H. (2009). Catching fly balls in virtual reality: A critical test of the outfielder problem. *Journal of Vision*, 9(13), 14–14. doi:10.1167/9.13.14

Floreano, D., Ijspeert, A. J., & Schaal, S. (2014). Robotics and neuroscience. *Curr Biol*, 24(18), R910–R920. doi:10.1016/j.cub.2014.07.058

Floreano, D., Zufferey, J.-C., Klaptocz, A., Germann, J., & Kovac, M. (2017). Aerial locomotion in cluttered environments. In *Robotics Research* (Vol. 100 2, pp. 21–39). Cham: Springer. doi:10.1007/978-3-319-29363-9_2

Fukusima, S. S., Loomis, J. M., & Da Silva, J. A. (1997). Visual perception of egocentric distance as assessed by triangulation. *Journal of Experimental Psychology: Human Perception and Performance*, 23(1), 86.

Ghose, K., Horiuchi, T. K., Krishnaprasad, P. S., & Moss, C. F. (2006). Echolocating Bats Use a Nearly Time-Optimal Strategy to Intercept Prey. *PLoS Biology*, 4(5), e108.

Gibson, J. J. (1950). *The Perception of the Visual World*. Cambridge: The Riverside Press.

Gibson, J. J. (1958). Visually controlled locomotion and visual orientation in animals. *British Journal of Psychology*, 49(3), 182–194. doi:10.1111/j.2044-8295.1958.tb00656.x

Gibson, J. J. (1979). The Ecological Approach to Visual Perception Текст. doi:10.4324/9781315740218-10

Gibson, J. J. (1977). The theory of affordances. *Hilldale, USA*, 1(2).

Gibson, J. J., Olum, P., & Rosenblatt, F. (1955). Parallax and perspective during aircraft landings. *The American Journal of Psychology*, 68(3), 372–385.

Gibson, J. J. (1966). The senses considered as perceptual systems.

Godthelp, H. (1986). Vehicle control during curve driving. *Human Factors*, 28 (2), 211–221.

Godthelp, J. (1985). Precognitive control: Open-and closed-loop steering in a lane-change manoeuvre. *Ergonomics*, 28(10), 1419–1438.

Graziano, M. S., Andersen, R. A., & Snowden, R. J. (1994). Tuning of MST neurons to spiral motions. *Journal of Neuroscience*, 14(1), 54–67.

Greenlee, M. W., Frank, S. M., Kaliuzhna, M., Blanke, O., Bremmer, F., Churan, J., . . . Smith, A. T. (2016). Multisensory integration in self motion perception. *Multisensory Research*, 29(6–7), 525–556.

Gu, Y., Angelaki, D. E., & Deangelis, G. C. (2008). Neural correlates of multi-sensory cue integration in macaque MSTd. *Nat Neurosci*, 11(10), 1201–1210. doi:10.1038/nn.2191

Gu, Y., DeAngelis, G. C., & Angelaki, D. E. (2007). A functional link between area MSTd and heading perception based on vestibular signals. *Nat Neurosci*, 10(8), 1038–1047. doi:10.1038/nn1935

Gu, Y., Deangelis, G. C., & Angelaki, D. E. (2012). Causal links between dorsal medial superior temporal area neurons and multisensory heading perception. *J Neurosci*, 32(7), 2299–2313. doi:10.1523/JNEUROSCI.5154-11.2012

Hayhoe, M. M. (2017). Vision and action. *Annual Review of Vision Science*, 3, 389–413.

Hildreth, E. C., Beusmans, J. M. H., Boer, E. R., & Royden, C. S. (2000). From vision to action: Experiments and models of steering control during driving. *Journal of Experimental Psychology: Human Perception and Performance*, 26(3), 1106.

Hsu, J. (2019). Machines on mission possible. *Nature Machine Intelligence*, 1 (3), 124–127. doi:10.1038/s42256-019-0034-3

Israël, I., & Warren, W. H. (2005). Vestibular, proprioceptive, and visual influences on the perception of orientation and self-motion in humans. Head direction cells and the neural mechanisms of spatial orientation, 347–381.

Jirsa, V. K., & Kelso, S. (2004). *Coordination dynamics: Issues and trends*. Springer Science & Business Media.

Kaiser, M. K., & Mowafy, L. (1993). Optical specification of time-to-passage: Observers' sensitivity to global tau. *Journal of Experimental Psychology: Human Perception and Performance*, 19(5), 1028.

Kelly, J. W., Loomis, J. M., & Beall, A. C. (2005). The importance of perceived relative motion in the control of posture. *Exp Brain Res*, 161(3), 285–292. doi:10.1007/s00221-004-2069-9

Kelso, J. A. S. (1995). *Dynamic Patterns: The Self-Organization of Brain and Behavior*. Massachusetts Institute of Technology Press.

Kim, N.-G., & Turvey, M. T. (1999). Eye movements and a rule for perceiving direction of heading. *Ecological Psychology*, 11(3), 233–248.

Konczak, J., Meeuwsen, H. J., & Cress, M. E. (1992). Changing affordances in stair climbing: The perception of maximum climbability in young and older adults. *Journal of Experimental Psychology: Human Perception and Performance*, 18(3), 691.

Kuo, A. D., & Donelan, J. M. (2010). Dynamic principles of gait and their clinical implications. *Physical Therapy*, 90(2), 157–174.

Lappe, M., Bremmer, F., & Van den Berg, A. V. (1999). Perception of self-motion from visual flow. *Trends in Cognitive Sciences*, 3(9), 329–336.

Lappi, O., & Mole, C. (2018). Visuomotor control, eye movements, and steering: A unified approach for incorporating feedback, feedforward, and internal models. *Psychological Bulletin*, 144(10), 981–1001. doi:10.1037/bul0000150

Latash, M. L. (2008). *Synergy*. Oxford University Press.

Layton, O. W., & Fajen, B. R. (2016a). A neural model of MST and MT explains perceived object motion during self-motion. *Journal of Neuroscience*, 36 (31), 8093–8102. doi:10.1523/JNEUROSCI.4593-15.2016

Layton, O. W., & Fajen, B. R. (2016b). Competitive dynamics in MSTd: A mechanism for robust heading perception based on optic flow. *PLoS Computational Biology*, 12(6).

Layton, O. W., & Fajen, B. R. (2016c). Sources of bias in the perception of heading in the presence of moving objects: Object-based and border-based discrepancies. *J Vis*, 16(1), 9. doi:10.1167/16.1.9

Layton, O. W., & Fajen, B. R. (2016d). The temporal dynamics of heading perception in the presence of moving objects. *J Neurophysiol*, 115(1), 286–300. doi:10.1152/jn.00866.2015

Layton, O. W., & Fajen, B. R. (2017). Possible role for recurrent interactions between expansion and contraction cells in MSTd during self-motion perception in dynamic environments. *J Vis*, 17(5), 5. doi:10.1167/17.5.5

Layton, O. W., Mingolla, E., & Browning, N. A. (2012). A motion pooling model of visually guided navigation explains human behavior in the presence of independently moving objects. *Journal of Vision*, 12(1), 20–20. doi:10.1167/12.1.20

Lee, D. N. (1980). Visuo-motor coordination in space-time. In G. E. Stelmach & J. Requin (Eds.), *Tutorials in Motor Behavior* (pp. 281–295). Amsterdam: North-Holland. doi:10.1111/j.1467-9450.1977.tb00281.x

Lee, D. N. (1976). A theory of visual control of braking based on information about time-to-collision. *Perception*, 5(4), 437–459. doi:10.1068/p050437

Lee, D. N. (1974). Visual information during locomotion. In MacLeod, H. & Pick, H. (Eds.) Perception: Essays in Honor of J. J. Gibson, Ithaca: Cornell University Press.

Lee, D. N., Lishman, J. R., & Thomson, J. A. (1982). Regulation of gait in long jumping. *Journal of Experimental Psychology: Human Perception and Performance*, 8(3), 448–459.

Lenoir, M., Musch, E., Janssens, M., Thiery, E., & Uyttenhove, J. (1999). Intercepting moving objects during self-motion. *Journal of Motor Behavior*, 31(1), 55–67.

Li, L., Chen, J., & Peng, X. (2009). Influence of visual path information on human heading perception during rotation. *Journal of Vision*, 9(3):29, 1–14. doi:10.1167/9.3.29

Li, L., & Cheng, J. C. (2011). Perceiving path from optic flow. *Journal of Vision*, 11(1). doi:10.1167/11.1.22

Li, L., Ni, L., Lappe, M., Niehorster, D. C., & Sun, Q. (2018). No special treatment of independent object motion for heading perception. *Journal of Vision*, 18(4), 19–16. doi:10.1167/18.4.19

Li, L., Stone, L. S., & Chen, J. (2011). Influence of optic-flow information beyond the velocity field on the active control of heading. *Journal of Vision*, 11(4), 9–9. doi:10.1167/11.4.9

Li, L., Sweet, B. T., & Stone, L. S. (2006). Humans can perceive heading without visual path information. *Journal of Vision*, 6(9), 2–2. doi:10.1167/6.9.2

Li, L., & Warren, W. H. (2000). Perception of heading during rotation: Sufficiency of dense motion parallax and reference objects. *Vision Research*, 40(28), 3873–3894.

Longuet-Higgins, H. C., & Prazdny, K. (1980). The interpretation of a moving retinal image. *Proceedings of the Royal Society of London. Series B. Biological Sciences*, 208(1173), 385–397.

Loomis, J. M., & Beall, A. C. (1998). Visually controlled locomotion: Its dependence on optic flow, three-dimensional space perception, and cognition. *Ecological Psychology*, 10(3–4), 271–285.

Loomis, J. M., & Beall, A. C. (2004). Model-based control of perception/action. In *Optic Flow and Beyond* (pp. 421–441). Dordrecht: Springer.

Loomis, J. M., Da Silva, J. A., Fujita, N., & Fukusima, S. S. (1992). Visual space perception and visually directed action. *Journal of Experimental Psychology: Human Perception and Performance*, 18(4), 906.

Macuga, K. L., Beall, A. C., Smith, R. S., & Loomis, J. M. (2019). Visual control of steering in curve driving. *Journal of Vision*, 19(5), 1–1. doi:10.1167/19.5.1

Mark, L. S. (1987). Eyeheight-scaled information about affordances: A study of sitting and stair climbing. *Journal of Experimental Psychology: Human Perception and Performance*, 13(3), 361–370.

Mark, L. S., Balliett, J. A., Craver, K. D., Douglas, S. D., & Fox, T. (1990). What an actor must do in order to perceive the affordance for sitting. *Ecological Psychology*, 2(4), 325–366.

Matthis, J. S., Muller, K. S., Bonnen, K., & Hayhoe, M. M. (2020). Retinal optic flow during natural locomotion. doi:10.1101/2020.07.23.217893

McNamee, D., & Wolpert, D. M. (2019). Internal models in biological control. *Annual Review of Control, Robotics, and Autonomous Systems*, 2, 339–364.

Michaels, C. F., & Oudejans, R. R. D. (1992). The optics and actions of catching fly balls: Zeroing out optical acceleration. *Ecological Psychology*, 4(4), 199–222. doi:10.1207/s15326969eco0404_1

Michaels, C. F., Prindle, S., & Turvey, M. T. (1985). A note on the natural basis of action categories: The catching distance of mantids. *Journal of Motor Behavior*, 17(2), 255–264. doi:10.1080/00222895.1985.10735348

Mischiati, M., Lin, H. T., Herold, P., Imler, E., Olberg, R., & Leonardo, A. (2015). Internal models direct dragonfly interception steering. *Nature*, 517 (7534), 333–338. doi:10.1038/nature14045

Mohler, B. J., Thompson, W. B., Creem-Regehr, S. H., Willemsen, P., Pick, J., Herbert L., & Rieser, J. J. (2007). Calibration of locomotion resulting from visual motion in a treadmill-based virtual environment. *ACM Transactions on Applied Perception (TAP)*, 4(1), 4–es.

Mole, C. D., Lappi, O., Giles, O., Markkula, G., Mars, F., & Wilkie, R. M. (2019). Getting Back Into the Loop: The Perceptual-Motor Determinants of Successful Transitions out of Automated Driving. Hum Factors, 18720819829594. doi:10.1177/0018720819829594

Morice, A. H. P., François, M., Jacobs, D. M., & Montagne, G. (2010). Environmental constraints modify the way an interceptive action is controlled. *Experimental Brain Research*, 202(2), 397–411. doi:10.1007/s00221-009-2147-0

Olberg, R. M., Worthington, A. H., Fox, J. L., Bessette, C. E., & Loosemore, M. P. (2005). Prey size selection and distance estimation in foraging adult dragonflies. *J Comp Physiol A Neuroethol Sens Neural Behav Physiol*, 191 (9), 791–797. doi:10.1007/s00359-005-0002-8

Olberg, R. M., Worthington, A. H., & Venator, K. R. (2000). Prey pursuit and interception in dragonflies. *Journal of Comparative Physiology A: Sensory,*

Neural, and Behavioral Physiology, 186(2), 155–162. doi:10.1007/s003590050015

Oudejans, R. R., Michaels, C. F., van Dort, B., & Frissen, E. J. P. (1996). To cross or not to cross: The effect of locomotion on street-crossing behavior. *Ecological Psychology*, 8(3), 259–267. doi:10.1207/s15326969eco0803_4

Oudejans, R. R. D., Michaels, C. F., Bakker, F. C., & Dolné, M. A. (1996). The relevance of action in perceiving affordances: Perception of catchableness of fly balls. *Journal of Experimental Psychology: Human Perception and Performance*, 22(4), 879–891.

Perrone, J. A. (2018). Visual-vestibular estimation of the body's curvilinear motion through the world: A computational model. *J Vis*, 18(4), 1. doi:10.1167/18.4.1

Perrone, J. A. (1992). Model for the computation of self-motion in biological systems. *JOSA A*, 9(2), 177–194.

Philbeck, J. W., Loomis, J. M., & Beall, A. C. (1997). Visually perceived location is an invariant in the control of action. *Perception & Psychophysics*, 59(4), 601–612.

Plumert, J. M., & Kearney, J. K. (2014). How do children perceive and act on dynamic affordances in crossing traffic-filled roads. *Child Dev Perspect*, 8(4), 207–212. doi:10.1111/cdep.12089

Postma, D. B. W. (2019). *Affordance-based control in running to catch fly balls*. Ph.D. thesis, University of Groningen.

Postma, D. B. W., Lemmink, K. A. P. M., & Zaal, F. T. J. M. (2018). The affordance of catchability in running to intercept fly balls. *Journal of Experimental Psychology: Human Perception and Performance*, 44(9), 1336–1347. doi:10.1037/xhp0000531

Postma, D. B. W., Smith, J., Pepping, G.-J., van Andel, S., & Zaal, F. T. J. M. (2017). When a fly ball is out of reach: Catchability judgments are not based on optical acceleration cancelation. *Frontiers in Psychology*, 8(868), 1427–1428. doi:10.3389/fpsyg.2017.00535

Raudies, F., & Neumann, H. (2013). Modeling heading and path perception from optic flow in the case of independently moving objects. *Frontiers in Behavioral Neuroscience*, 7, 23. doi:10.3389/fnbeh.2013.00023

Reed, E. S. (1988). *James J. Gibson and the Psychology of Perception*. Yale University Press.

Regan, D., & Beverley, K. I. (1982). How do we avoid confounding the direction we are looking and the direction we are moving. *Science*, 215 (4529), 194–196.

Riddell, H., Li, L., & Lappe, M. (2019). Heading perception from optic flow in the presence of biological motion. *J Vis*, 19(14), 25. doi:10.1167/19.14.25

Rieger, J. H. (1983). Information in optical flows induced by curved paths of observation. *JOSA*, 73(3), 339–344. doi:10.1364/JOSA.73.000339

Rieger, J. H., & Lawton, D. T. (1985). Processing differential image motion. *JOSA A*, 2, 354–359.

Rieser, J. J., Ashmead, D. H., Talor, C. R., & Youngquist, G. A. (1990). Visual perception and the guidance of locomotion without vision to previously seen targets. *Perception*, 19(5), 675–689. doi:10.1068/p190675

Rieser, J. J., Pick, H. L., Ashmead, D. H., & Garing, A. E. (1995). Calibration of human locomotion and models of perceptual-motor organization. *Journal of Experimental Psychology: Human Perception and Performance*, 21(3), 480.

Rio, K. W., Rhea, C. K., & Warren, W. H. (2014). Follow the leader: Visual control of speed in pedestrian following. *J Vis*, 14(2). doi:10.1167/14.2.4

Royden, C. S. (1994). Analysis of misperceived observer motion during simulated eye rotations. *Vision Research*, 34(23), 3215–3222. doi:10.1016/0042-6989(94)90085-X

Royden, C. S., Banks, M. S., & Crowell, J. A. (1992). The perception of heading during eye movements. *Nature*, 360(6404), 583–585.

Royden, C. S., Crowell, J. A., & Banks, M. S. (1994). Estimating heading during eye movements. *Vision Research*, 34(23), 3197–3214. doi:10.1016/0042-6989(94)90084-1

Royden, C. S., & Hildreth, E. C. (1996). Human heading judgments in the presence of moving objects. *Perception & Psychophysics*, 58(6), 836–856.

Rushton, S. K., Chen, R., & Li, L. (2018). Ability to identify scene-relative object movement is not limited by, or yoked to, ability to perceive heading. *Journal of Vision*, 18(6), 11–11. doi:10.1167/18.6.11

Rushton, S. K., Harris, J. M., Lloyd, M. R., & Wann, J. P. (1998). Guidance of locomotion on foot uses perceived target location rather than optic flow. *Current Biology*, 8(21), 1191–1194. doi:10.1016/S0960-9822(07)00492-7

Saito, H.- a., Yukie, M. , Tanaka, K. , Hikosaka, K. , Fukada, Y. , & Iwai, E. (1986). Integration of direction signals of image motion in the superior temporal sulcus of the macaque monkey. *Journal of Neuroscience*, 6(1), 145–157.

Saunders, J. A. (2010). View rotation is used to perceive path curvature from optic flow. *Journal of Vision*, 10(13), 25–25. doi:10.1167/10.7.806

Saunders, J. A., & Ma, K.-Y. (2011). Can observers judge future circular path relative to a target from retinal flow? *Journal of Vision*, 11(7), 16–16. doi:10.1167/11.7.16

Senders, J. W., Kristofferson, A. B., Levison, W. H., Dietrich, C. W., & Ward, J. L. (1967). The attentional demand of automobile driving. Highway Research Record, 195, 15-33.

Srinivasan, M. V. (2011). Visual control of navigation in insects and its relevance for robotics. *Current Opinion in Neurobiology*, 21(4), 535–543. doi:10.1016/j.conb.2011.05.020

Steinmetz, S. T., Layton, O. W., Powell, N. V., & Fajen, B. R. (2020). Affordance-based versus current-future accounts of choosing whether to pursue or abandon the chase of a moving target. *J Vis*, 20(3), 8. doi:10.1167/jov.20.3.8

Stoffregen, T. A., Yang, C.-M., Giveans, M. R., Flanagan, M., & Bardy, B. G. (2009). Movement in the perception of an affordance for wheelchair locomotion. *Ecological Psychology*, 21(1), 1–36.

Stone, L. S., & Perrone, J. A. (1997). Human heading estimation during visually simulated curvilinear motion. *Vision Research*, 37(5), 573–590. doi:10.1016/S0042-6989(96)00204-0

Strogatz, S. (2001). Nonlinear dynamics and chaos: with applications to physics, biology, chemistry, and engineering (studies in nonlinearity).

Sunkara, A., DeAngelis, G. C., & Angelaki, D. E. (2016). Joint representation of translational and rotational components of optic flow in parietal cortex. *Proceedings of the National Academy of Sciences of the United States of America*, 113(18), 5077–5082. doi:10.1073/pnas.1604818113

Tanaka, K., & Saito, H.-A. (1989). Analysis of motion of the visual field by direction, expansion/contraction, and rotation cells clustered in the dorsal part of the medial superior temporal area of the macaque monkey. *Journal of Neurophysiology*, 62(3), 626–641.

Thomson, J. A. (1983). Is continuous visual monitoring necessary in visually guided locomotion. *Journal of Experimental Psychology: Human Perception and Performance*, 9(3), 427.

Turvey, M. T. (1990). Coordination. *American Psychologist*, 45(8), 938.

Turvey, M. T. (2007). Action and perception at the level of synergies. *Human Movement Science*, 26(4), 657–697.

Turvey, M. T., & Carello, C. (1996). Dynamics of Bernstein's level of synergies. Dexterity and its development, 339–376.

van Andel, S., Cole, M. H., & Pepping, G.-J. (2017). A systematic review on perceptual-motor calibration to changes in action capabilities. *Human Movement Science*, 51, 59–71. doi:10.1016/j.humov.2016.11.004

Van den Berg, A. V., & Brenner, E. (1994a). Humans combine the optic flow with static depth cues for robust perception of heading. *Vision Research*, 34(16), 2153–2167. doi:10.1016/0042-6989(94)90324-7

Van den Berg, A. V., & Brenner, E. (1994b). Why two eyes are better than one for judgements of heading. *Nature*, 371(6499), 700–702. doi:10.1038/371700a0

Wallis, G., Chatziastros, A., & Bülthoff, H. (2002a). An unexpected role for visual feedback in vehicle steering control. *Current Biology*, 12(4), 295–299. doi:10.1016/S0960-9822(02)00685-1

Wallis, G., Chatziastros, A., & Bülthoff, H. (2002b). An unexpected role for visual feedback in vehicle steering control. *Current Biology*, 12(4), 295–299.

Wann, J., & Land, M. (2000). Steering with or without the flow: Is the retrieval of heading necessary? *Trends in Cognitive Sciences*, 4(8), 319–324. doi:10.1016/S1364-6613(00)01513-8

Wann, J. P., & Swapp, D. K. (2000). Why you should look where you are going. *Nature Neuroscience*, 3 (7), 647.

Warren, P., & Rushton, S. (2007). Perception of object trajectory: Parsing retinal motion into self and object. *Journal of Vision*.

Warren, P., & Rushton, S. (2009a). Perception of scene-relative object movement: Optic flow parsing and the . . . . *Vision Research*.

Warren, P. A., & Rushton, S. K. (2009b). Optic flow processing for the assessment of object movement during ego movement. *Current Biology*, 19(18), 1555–1560. doi:10.1016/j.cub.2009.07.057

Warren, P. A., Rushton, S. K., & Foulkes, A. J. (2012). Does optic flow parsing depend on prior estimation of heading? *Journal of Vision*, 12(11), 8.

Warren, W. H. (1984). Perceiving affordances: Visual guidance of stair climbing. *Journal of Experimental Psychology: Human Perception and Performance*, 10(5), 683–703.

Warren, W. H. (1988). Action modes and laws of control for the visual guidance of action. In *Complex Movement Behavior: The Motor-Action Controversy* (pp. 339–380). Elsevier.

Warren, W. H. (1995). Self-motion: Visual perception and visual control. In *Perception of Space and Motion* (pp. 263–325). Elsevier.

Warren, W. H. (1998a). The state of flow. High-Level Motion Processing: Computational, Neurobiological and Psychophysical Perspectives, 315–358.

Warren, W. H. (1998b). Visually controlled locomotion: 40 years later. *Ecological Psychology*, 10 (3–4), 177–219.

Warren, W. H. (2004). Optic flow. In L. Chalupa & J. Werner (eds.), *The Visual Neurosciences* (pp. 1247–1259). Cambridge, MA: Massachusetts Institute of Technology Press.

Warren, W. H. (2006). The dynamics of perception and action. *Psychological Review*, 113(2), 358–389.

Warren, W. H. (2007). Action-scaled information for the visual control of locomotion. Closing the gap: The scientific writings of David N. Lee, 243–258.

Warren, W. H. (2018). Collective motion in human crowds. *Current Directions in Psychological Science*, 12, 096372141774674–096372141774679. doi:10.1177/0963721417746743

Warren, W. H., Blackwell, A. W., Kurtz, K. J., Hatsopoulos, N. G., & Kalish, M. L. (1991). On the sufficiency of the velocity field for perception of heading. *Biological Cybernetics*, 65(5), 311–320.

Warren, W. H., & Fajen, B. R. (2004). From optic flow to laws of control. In *Optic Flow and Beyond* (pp. 307–337). Springer.

Warren, W. H., & Fajen, B. R. (2008). Behavioral dynamics of visually guided locomotion. In *Coordination: Neural, Behavioral and Social Dynamics* (pp. 45–75). Springer.

Warren, W. H., & Hannon, D. J. (1988). Direction of self-motion is perceived from optical flow. *Nature*, 336(6195), 162–163. doi:10.1038/336162a0

Warren, W. H., Kay, B. A., Zosh, W. D., Duchon, A. P., & Sahuc, S. (2001). Optic flow is used to control human walking. *Nature Neuroscience*, 4(2), 213. doi:10.1038/84054

Warren, W. H., Mestre, D. R., Blackwell, A. W., & Morris, M. W. (1991). Perception of circular heading from optical flow. *Journal of Experimental Psychology: Human Perception and Performance*, 17(1), 28.

Warren, W. H., Morris, M. W., & Kalish, M. (1988). Perception of translational heading from optical flow. *Journal of Experimental Psychology: Human Perception and Performance*, 14(4), 646.

Warren, W. H., & Saunders, J. A. (1995). Perceiving heading in the presence of moving objects. *Perception*, 24(3), 315–331. doi:10.1068/p240315

Warren, W. H., & Whang, S. (1987). Visual guidance of walking through apertures: Body-scaled information for affordances. *Journal of Experimental Psychology: Human Perception and Performance*, 13(3), 371–383.

Warren, W. H., Young, D. S., & Lee, D. N. (1986). Visual control of step length during running over irregular terrain. *Journal of Experimental Psychology: Human Perception and Performance*, 12(3), 259–266. doi:10.1037/0096-1523.12.3.259

Wilkie, R. M., & Wann, J. P. (2006). Judgments of path, not heading, guide locomotion. *Journal of Experimental Psychology: Human Perception and Perfo -rmance*, 32(1), 88.

Wraga, M. (1999a). The role of eye height in perceiving affordances and object dimensions. *Perception & Psychophysics*, 61(3), 490–507.

Wraga, M. (1999b). Using eye height in different postures to scale the heights of objects. *Journal of Experimental Psychology: Human Perception and Performance*, 25(2), 518.

Yilmaz, E. H., & Warren, W. H. (1995). Visual control of braking: A test of the !τ hypothesis. *Journal of Experimental Psychology: Human Perception and Performance*, 21(5), 996.

Zhao, H., Straub, D., & Rothkopf, C. A. (2019). The visual control of interceptive steering: How do people steer a car to intercept a moving target. *J Vis*, 19(14), 11. doi:10.1167/19.14.11

Zhao, H., & Warren, W. H. (2015). Online and model-based approaches to the visual control of action. *Vision Research*, 110(PB), 190–202. doi:10.1016/j.visres.2014.10.008

Zhao, H., & Warren, W. H. (2017). *Intercepting a moving target in fog: Online or model-based control?* 17, 1–13. doi:10.1167/17.5.12.doi

Cambridge Elements ≡

Perception

James T. Enns
The University of British Columbia

Editor James T. Enns is Professor at the University of British Columbia, where he researches the interaction of perception, attention, emotion, and social factors. He has previously been Editor of the *Journal of Experimental Psychology: Human Perception and Performance* and an Associate Editor at *Psychological Science, Consciousness and Cognition, Attention Perception & Psychophysics,* and *Visual Cognition.*

Editorial Board

About the Series

The modern study of human perception includes event perception, bidirectional influences between perception and action, music, language, the integration of the senses, human action observation, and the important roles of emotion, motivation, and social factors. Each Element in the series combines authoritative literature reviews of foundational topics with forward-looking presentations of the recent developments on a given topic.

Cambridge Elements ≡

Perception

Elements in the Series

Hypothesis Testing Reconsidered
Gregory Francis

Chemical Senses in Feeding, Belonging, and Surviving: Or, Are You Going to Eat That?
Paul A. S. Breslin

Multisensory Interactions in the Real World
Salvador Soto-Faraco, Daria Kvasova, Emmanuel Biau, Nara Ikumi, Manuela Ruzzoli, Luis Morís-Fernández and Mireia Torralba

Human Color Vision and Tetrachromacy
Kimberly A. Jameson, Timothy A. Satalich, Kirbi C. Joe, Vladimir A. Bochko, Shari R. Atilano and M. Cristina Kenney

The Breadth of Visual Attention
Stephanie C. Goodhew

Attentional Selection: Top-Down, Bottom-Up and History-Based Biases
Jan Theeuwes and Michel Failing

Crossmodal Attention Applied: Lessons for Driving
Charles Spence and Salvador Soto-Faraco

Competition and Control during Working Memory
Anastasia Kiyonaga and Mark D'Esposito

Visual Control of Locomotion
Brett R. Fajen

A full series listing is available at: www.cambridge.org/EPER

Printed in the United States
by Baker & Taylor Publisher Services